Building Serverless Applications with Python

Develop fast, scalable, and cost-effective web applications that are always available

Jalem Raj Rohit

BIRMINGHAM - MUMBAI

Building Serverless Applications with Python

Commissioning Editor: Merint Mathew
Acquisition Editor: Sandeep Mishra
Content Development Editor: Rohit Kumar Singh
Technical Editor: Ruvika Rao
Copy Editor: Safis Editing
Project Coordinator: Vaidehi Sawant
Proofreader: Safis Editing
Indexer: Priyanka Dhadke
Graphics: Jason Monteiro
Production Coordinator: Arvindkumar Gupta

First published: April 2018

Production reference: 1190418

Published by Packt Publishing Ltd.
Livery Place
35 Livery Street
Birmingham
B3 2PB, UK.

ISBN 978-1-78728-867-6

www.packtpub.com

`mapt.io`

Mapt is an online digital library that gives you full access to over 5,000 books and videos, as well as industry leading tools to help you plan your personal development and advance your career. For more information, please visit our website.

Why subscribe?

- Spend less time learning and more time coding with practical eBooks and Videos from over 4,000 industry professionals

- Improve your learning with Skill Plans built especially for you

- Get a free eBook or video every month

- Mapt is fully searchable

- Copy and paste, print, and bookmark content

PacktPub.com

Did you know that Packt offers eBook versions of every book published, with PDF and ePub files available? You can upgrade to the eBook version at `www.PacktPub.com` and as a print book customer, you are entitled to a discount on the eBook copy. Get in touch with us at `service@packtpub.com` for more details.

At `www.PacktPub.com`, you can also read a collection of free technical articles, sign up for a range of free newsletters, and receive exclusive discounts and offers on Packt books and eBooks.

Contributors

About the author

Jalem Raj Rohit is an IIT Jodhpur graduate with a keen interest in recommender systems, machine learning, and serverless and distributed systems. Raj currently works as a senior consultant—data science—and NLP at Episource, before which he worked at Zomato and Kayako. He contributes to open source projects in Python, Go, and Julia. He also speaks at tech conferences about serverless engineering and machine learning.

About the reviewer

Sanjeev Jaiswal is a computer graduate from CUSAT with 9 years of industrial experience. He basically uses Perl, Python, AWS, and GNU/Linux for his day-to-day activities. He is currently working on projects involving penetration testing, source code review, security design and implementations in AWS, and cloud security projects.

He is learning DevSecOps and Security Automation currently as well. Sanjeev loves teaching engineering students and IT professionals. He has been teaching in his leisure time for the last 8 years.

Special thanks to my wife, Shalini Jaiswal, for her unconditional support, and my friends Ranjan, Ritesh, Mickey, Shankar, and Santosh for their care and support all the time. Thanks to the people at Packt for the project and the opportunity to learn good stuff from skilled professionals through reviewing the project.

Packt is searching for authors like you

If you're interested in becoming an author for Packt, please visit authors.packtpub.com and apply today. We have worked with thousands of developers and tech professionals, just like you, to help them share their insight with the global tech community. You can make a general application, apply for a specific hot topic that we are recruiting an author for, or submit your own idea.

Table of Contents

Preface

Serverless engineering is a new domain of engineering that allows developers to write code and deploy infrastructures without having to worry about maintaining servers. This book explains the concepts of serverless engineering with Python examples on cloud architectures.

Who this book is for

This book is for Python developers who would like to learn about serverless architectures in cloud-based platforms such as Azure and Amazon Web Services (AWS). Python programming knowledge is assumed.

What this book covers

Chapter 1, *The Serverless Paradigm*, introduces the reader to the concepts of microservices and serverless architectures, and provides a clear understanding of the pros and cons.

Chapter 2, *Building a Serverless Application in AWS*, covers AWS Lambda and explains the concepts, workings, and the components involved in the tool in detail. It also explains the nuances involved in security, user controls, and versioning code inside Lambda.

Chapter 3, *Setting Up Serverless Architectures*, goes into further detail about the various triggers in AWS Lambda and how they integrate with the functions. The reader will learn what the event structure of each trigger will look like and how to modify the Lambda function with respect to the type of trigger used.

Chapter 4, *Deploying Serverless APIs*, explores the AWS API Gateway and also teaches the reader how to build efficient, scalable serverless APIs using the API Gateway and Lambda. It goes on to teach the reader how to improve the API by adding authorization and how to set up user-level controls such as throttling of requests.

Chapter 5, *Logging and Monitoring*, presents the concept of logging and monitoring in serverless applications. This is mostly still an unsolved problem in this domain. This chapter guides the reader through setting up logging and monitoring in the AWS environment with Python via custom metrics and logging. This chapter also goes into the details of best practices when it comes to logging and monitoring Lambda functions in Python.

Chapter 6, *Scaling Up Serverless Architectures*, discusses the practice of scaling up serverless architectures for large workloads using several third-party tools. This chapter also teaches the reader how to handle security, logging, and monitoring using the available Python modules.

Chapter 7, *Security in AWS Lambda*, teaches readers to deploy secure serverless applications by leveraging the AWS security features available. This involves having strict controls on components that the application can access, on the users who can handle or access the application, and so on. This also involves understanding AWS virtual private clouds and subnets for an in-depth understanding of the security features and best practices you can follow in AWS Lambda.

Chapter 8, *Deploying a Lambda Function with SAM*, looks at how to deploy Lambda functions as infrastructure as code via the Serverless Application Model, which is a new way of writing and deploying Lambda functions that makes it easier to integrate with other IaaS services, such as CloudFormation.

Chapter 9, *Introduction to Microsoft Azure Functions*, familiarizes the reader with Microsoft Azure Functions, and explains how to configure and understand the components of the tool.

To get the most out of this book

The reader should be comfortable with the Python programming language. So, prior experience with it is expected. Prior experience with cloud-based systems will also be helpful.

Conventions used

There are a number of text conventions used throughout this book.

CodeInText: Indicates code words in text, database table names, folder names, filenames, file extensions, pathnames, dummy URLs, user input, and Twitter handles. Here is an example: "It is to be noted that the meta information should always be included for all SAM, which includes AWSTemplateFormatVersion and Transform. This would tell CloudFormation that the code you have written is an AWS SAM code and a serverless application."

A block of code is set as follows:

```
AWSTemplateFormatVersion: '2010-09-09'
Transform: AWS::Serverless-2016-10-31
```

Bold: Indicates a new term, an important word, or words that you see onscreen. For example, words in menus or dialog boxes appear in the text like this. Here is an example: "For creating a function, you need to click on the orange **Create a function** button on the right."

 Warnings or important notes appear like this.

 Tips and tricks appear like this.

Get in touch

Feedback from our readers is always welcome.

General feedback: Email `feedback@packtpub.com` and mention the book title in the subject of your message. If you have questions about any aspect of this book, please email us at `questions@packtpub.com`.

Errata: Although we have taken every care to ensure the accuracy of our content, mistakes do happen. If you have found a mistake in this book, we would be grateful if you would report this to us. Please visit `www.packtpub.com/submit-errata`, selecting your book, clicking on the Errata Submission Form link, and entering the details.

Piracy: If you come across any illegal copies of our works in any form on the Internet, we would be grateful if you would provide us with the location address or website name. Please contact us at `copyright@packtpub.com` with a link to the material.

If you are interested in becoming an author: If there is a topic that you have expertise in and you are interested in either writing or contributing to a book, please visit `authors.packtpub.com`.

Reviews

Please leave a review. Once you have read and used this book, why not leave a review on the site that you purchased it from? Potential readers can then see and use your unbiased opinion to make purchase decisions, we at Packt can understand what you think about our products, and our authors can see your feedback on their book. Thank you!

For more information about Packt, please visit packtpub.com.

The Serverless Paradigm 1

Most probably, if you are reading this book, you have already heard about the serverless paradigm and the terms serverless engineering and serverless architecture. Nowadays, the way developers deploy applications has changed drastically, especially in the domain of data engineering and web development, thanks to **event-based architectural designs**, also called **serverless architectures**.

It is not uncommon to have idle resources and servers in production idle after the server workload has finished, or waiting for the next workload to come. This introduces a bit of redundancy in the infrastructure. What if there was no need for idle resources lying around when there is no workload? What if resources can be created when necessary and be destroyed once the work is done?

At the end of this chapter, you will understand how serverless architectures and functions as a service work, and how you can build them into your existing software infrastructure. You will also learn what microservices are, and decide whether microservices or serverless operations are well-suited for your architecture or not. You will also learn how to build serverless applications with Python on major cloud service providers, such as **Amazon Web Services (AWS)** and **Microsoft's Azure**.

This chapter will cover the following points:

- Understanding serverless architectures
- Understanding microservices
- Serverless architectures don't have to be real-time only
- Pros and cons of serverless architectures

Understanding serverless architectures

The concept of serverless architectures or serverless engineering revolves entirely around understanding the concept of functions as a service. The most technical and accurate definition of serverless computing on the internet is as follows:

> *"Serverless computing, also known as **function as a service (FAAS)**, is a cloud computing and code execution model in which the cloud provider fully manages starting and stopping of a function's container **platform as a service (PaaS)**."*

Now, let's go into the details of each part of that definition to understand the paradigm of serverless computing better. We shall start with the term function as a service. It means that every serverless model has a function that is executed on the cloud. These functions are nothing but blocks of code, that are executed depending on the trigger that is associated with the function. This is a complete list of triggers in the AWS Lambda environment:

- Amazon S3
- Amazon DynamoDB
- Amazon Kinesis Streams
- Amazon Simple Notification Service
- Amazon Simple Email Service
- Amazon Cognito
- AWS CloudFormation
- Amazon CloudWatch Logs
- Amazon CloudWatch Events
- AWS CodeCommit
- Scheduled Events (powered by Amazon CloudWatch Events)
- AWS Config
- Amazon Alexa
- Amazon Lex
- Amazon API Gateway
- Other Event Sources: Invoking a Lambda Function On Demand
- Sample Events Published by Event Sources

Now let's understand what manages the starting and stopping of a function. Whenever a function is triggered via one of these available triggers, the cloud provider launches a container in which the function executes. Also, after the function is successfully executed the function has returned something, or if the function has run out of time, the container gets thatched away or destroyed. The thatching happens so that the container can be reused in the event of high demand and whenever there is very little time between two triggers. Now, we come to the next part of the sentence, the function's container. This means that the functions are launched and executed in containers. This is the standard definition of a container from Docker, a company that made the concept of containers very popular:

> *"A container image is a lightweight, stand-alone, executable package of a piece of software that includes everything needed to run it: code, runtime, system tools, system libraries, settings."*

This helps in packaging the code, the runtime environment, and so on of the function into a single deployment package for seamless execution. The **deployment package** contains the main code file for the function, all the non-standard libraries which are required for the function to execute. The creation process of a deployment package looks very similar to that of a virtual environment in Python.

So, we can clearly make out that there are no servers running round the clock in the case of serverless infrastructures. There is a clear benefit for this, which includes not having a dedicated Ops team member for monitoring the server boxes. So the extra member, if any, can focus on better things, such as software research, and so on. Not having servers running through the entire day saves a lot of money and resources for the company and/or personally. This benefit can be very clearly seen among machine learning and data engineering teams who make use of GPU instances for their regular workload. So having on-demand serverless GPU instances running, saves a lot of money without the developers or the Ops team needing to maintain them around the clock.

Understanding microservices

Similar to the concept of serverless, the design strategy, which is the microservice-oriented strategy, has also been very popular recently. This architecture design existed a long time before the idea of serverless came into existence though. Just as we tried to understand the serverless architectures from the technical definition on the internet, we shall try to do the same for microservices. The technical definition for microservices is:

> *"Microservices, also known as the **microservice architecture**, is an architectural style that structures an application as a collection of loosely coupled services, which implement business capabilities."*

Planning and designing the architecture in the form of microservices has its fair share of positives and negatives, just like serverless architectures. It's important to know about both, in order to appreciate and understand when and when not to leverage microservices in your existing architecture. Let's look at this and understand the positives of having microservice architectures, before moving over to the negatives.

Microservices help software teams stay agile, and improve incrementally. In simpler terms, as the services are decoupled from each other, it is very easy to upgrade and improve a service without causing the other to go down. For example, in social network software, if the chat and the feed are both microservices, then the feed doesn't have to go down when the software team are trying to upgrade or do minor fixes on the chat service. However, in large monolithic systems, it is difficult to break things up so easily in the way one can do with microservices. So, any fix or upgrade on even a small component of the architecture comes with downtime with the fix taking more time than intended.

The sheer size of the code base of monolithic architectures itself acts as a hindrance progress in the case of any small failures. Microservices, on the other hand, greatly help in boosting developer productivity by keeping code bases lean, so that they can fix and improve the service with very little or no overhead and downtime. Microservices can be much better leveraged via containers, which provide effective and complete virtual operating system environments, processes with isolation, and dedicated access to underlying hardware resources.

However, microservices come with their own bunch of disadvantages and downsides, the major one being having to deal with distributed systems. Now that each service is surviving on its own, the architect needs to figure out how each of them interacts with the others in order to make a fully functional product. So, proper co-ordination between the services and the decisions regarding how services move data between them is a very difficult choice that needs to be taken by the architect. Major distributed problems such as the *consensus*, the *CAP theorem*, and *maintaining the stability of consensus*, and the *connection*, are some issues that the engineer needs to handle while architecting for microservices. Ensuring and maintaining security is also a major problem in distributed systems and microservices. You needs to decide on separate security patterns and layers for each microservice, along with the security decisions necessary for the data interaction to happen between the services.

Serverless architectures don't have to be real-time only

Serverless architectures generally are leveraged as real-time systems as they work as a *function as service* which is triggered by a set of available triggers. However, this is a very common misconception, as serverless systems can be leveraged equally well both as real-time and batch architectures. Knowing how to leverage the concept of serverless systems as batch architectures will open up many engineering possibilities, as all engineering teams don't necessarily need or have real-time systems to operate.

Serverless systems can be batched by leveraging the following:

- The cron facility in triggers
- The concept of queues

Firstly, let's understand the concept of the **cron facility** in triggers. Serverless systems on the cloud have the ability to set up monitoring, which enables the trigger to get triggered every few minutes or hours and can be set as a normal cron job. This helps in leveraging the concept of serverless as a regular cron batch job. In the AWS environment, Lambda can be triggered as a cron via AWS CloudWatch, by setting the frequency of the cron by manually entering the time interval as the input and also by entering the interval in the cron format:

Example	Cron expression
Invoke Lambda function every 5 minutes	Copy rate(5 minutes)
Invoke Lambda function every hour	Copy rate(1 hour)
Invoke Lambda function every seven days	Copy rate(7 days)

One can also leverage the concept of queues when building serverless batch architectures. Let's understand this by setting an example data pipeline. Let's say the system which we intend to build does the following tasks:

1. A user or a service sends some data into a database or a much simpler data store, such as AWS's S3.
2. Once there are more than 100 files in my data store, we'll want to do some task. Let's say, doing some analytics on them, for example, such as counting the pages.

This can be achieved via queues, and this is one of the simpler serverless systems we can consider as an example. So, this can be achieved as follows:

1. The user or the service uploads or sends the data to the data store which we have selected.
2. A queue is configured for the purpose of this task.
3. An event can be configured to S3 buckets or data stores so that as soon as data enters into the store, a message is sent to the queue which we have configured earlier.
4. Monitoring systems can be set to monitor the queue for the number of messages in it. It is advisable to use the monitoring system of the cloud provider you are using so that the system stays completely serverless.
5. Alarms can be set to the monitoring systems, configuring a threshold for these alarms. For example, the alarm needs to be triggered whenever the number of messages in our queue reaches or exceeds 100.
6. This alarm can act as a trigger to the Lambda function which does the analytics by first receiving messages from the queue and then querying the data store using the filename received from the message.
7. Once the analytics are completed on the files, the processed files can be pushed to another data store for storage.
8. After the entire task is completed, the container or the server where the Lambda function has run will be terminated, thus making this pipeline completely serverless.

Pros and cons of serverless

As we now understand what serverless architectures and pipelines look like, how they may be leveraged into existing architectures, and also how microservices help keep architectures leaner and boost developer productivity, we shall look at the pros and cons of serverless systems in detail, so that software developers and architects can make decisions regarding when to leverage the serverless paradigm into their existing systems and when not to.

The positives of serverless systems are:

- **Lower infrastructure costs**: By deploying serverless systems, the infrastructure costs can be greatly optimized, as there would not be a need for servers to be running around the clock every day. As the servers start whenever the function is triggered, and stop whenever the function gets executed successfully, the billing would only be done for that brief time period when the function was running.
- **Less maintenance needed**: By virtue of the preceding reason, there is also no need for continuous monitoring and maintenance of servers. As the functions and triggers are automated, there is almost zero maintenance required for serverless systems.
- **Higher developer productivity**: As the developers don't need to worry about downtime and server maintenance, they can focus and work on better software challenges, such as scaling and designing functionalities.

The remaining part of the book will show you how serverless systems are changing the way software is done. So, as this chapter is intended to help architects decide whether serverless systems are a good choice for their architecture or not, we shall now look at the disadvantages of serverless systems.

The disadvantages of serverless systems are:

- **Time limit of the function**: The function which is whether executed, be it AWS's Lambda or GCP's cloud functions, has an upper time limit of 5 minutes. This makes execution of heavy computations impossible. However, this can be solved by executing a provisioning tool's playbook in nohup mode. This will be covered in detail, later in the chapter. However, making the playbook ready and setting up the container and anything else should be completed within the 5 minute time limit. The container gets automatically killed when the 5 minute limit is exceeded.

- **No control over the container environment**: The developer has no control over the environment of the container that is being created for executing the function. The operating system, the filesystem, and so on, are all decided by the cloud provider. For example, AWS's Lambda functions are executed inside containers that run the Amazon Linux operating system.
- **Monitoring containers**: Apart from the basic monitoring capabilities that are provided by the cloud provider via their in-house monitoring tools, there is no mechanism to do detailed monitoring of the container that is executing the serverless function. This becomes even more difficult when scaling up serverless systems to accommodate distributed systems.
- **No control on security**: There is no control on how the security of the data flow is ensured, as there is very little control over the container's environment. The container can be run in the VPC and subnets of the developer's choice, though, which helps work around this disadvantage.

However, serverless systems can be scaled up to distributed systems for large- scale computations where the developer need not worry about the time limit. As already mentioned, this will be discussed in detail in the upcoming chapters. However, for insight into an intuition on how one can choose serverless systems over monolithic systems for large-scale computations, let us understand some important pointers that need to be kept in mind when taking that architectural decision.

The pointers to be kept in mind when scaling serverless systems to distributed systems are:

- To scale up serverless systems into serverless distributed systems, one must understand how the concept of nohup works. It is a **POSIX** command that allows programs and processes to run in the background.
- Nohup processes should be properly logged, including both the output and the error logs. This is the only source of information for your processes.
- A provisioning tool, such as **Ansible** or **Chef** or a similar one, needs to be leveraged to create a master-workers architecture which has been spawned via the playbook running in nohup mode in the container where the serverless function is being executed.
- It is a good practice to ensure that all tasks that are being executed by the provisioning tool via the master server are properly monitored and logged, as there is no way one can retrieve the logs once the entire setup finishes executing.

- Proper security needs to be ensured by using a temporary credential facility available from the cloud providers.
- Proper closure should be ensured for the system. The workers and the master should self-terminate immediately after the pipeline of tasks finishes executing. This is very important and this is what makes the system serverless.
- Generally, temporary credentials come with an expiry time, which is 3,600 seconds for most environments. So, if the developer is using temporary credentials to execute a task which is supposed to take more than the expiry time, then there is a danger of the credentials getting expired.
- Debugging distributed serverless systems is an extremely difficult task for the following reasons:
  - Monitoring and debugging a nohup process is extremely difficult. Whenever you want to debug one, you have to either refer to the log file created by the process or kill the nohup process by using the process ID, and then manually run the scripts for debugging.
  - As the complete list of tasks executes sequentially in the provisioning tool, there is a danger that the instances may get terminated because the developer has forgotten to kill the nohup process before starting the debugging process.
  - As this is a distributed system, it goes without saying that the architecture should be able to self-heal in the case of any failure or a disaster. An example scenario can be when one of the workers goes down while performing some operation on a bunch of files. The entire bunch of files is now lost, and there is no means of recovery.
  - Another advanced disaster scenario can be when two worker servers go down while performing some operations on a bunch of files. In this case, the developer does not know which files have been executed successfully and which haven't.
- It is a good practice to ensure that all the worker instances receive an equal amount of the load to execute so that the load across the distributed system stays even and time and resources are well optimized.

Summary

In this chapter, we learned what serverless architecture is. Most importantly, the chapter helps architects decide if serverless is the way forward for their team and their engineering, and how to transition/migrate from their existing infrastructure to a serverless paradigm. We also looked at the paradigm of microservices and how they help make lightweight and highly agile architectures. This chapter also went into great detail about when a team should start thinking about microservices and when can they migrate or break their existing monolith(s) into microservices.

We then learned the art of building batch architectures in the serverless domain. One of the most common myths is that serverless systems are only for real-time computation purposes. However, we have learned how to leverage these systems for batch computations too, thus facilitating a whole lot of applications with the serverless paradigm. We looked at the pros and cons of going serverless so that better engineering decisions can be taken accordingly.

In the next chapter, we will cover a very detailed understanding of how AWS Lambda works, which is the core component of serverless engineering in the AWS cloud environment. We will understand how triggers work and how AWS Lambda functions work. You will learn about the concept of leveraging containers for executing serverless functions and the associated computational workload. Following that, we will also learn about configuring and testing Lambda functions, along with understanding the best practices while doing so. We will also cover versioning Lambda functions, in the same way versioning is done in code, and then create deployment packages for AWS Lambda, so that the developer can accommodate third-party libraries comfortably, along with the standard library ones.

2
Building a Serverless Application in AWS

This chapter will introduce the concept of serverless applications using AWS Lambda as the tool of choice. This will help you understand the concept, intuition, and working components involved in a serverless tool. It will also explain the nuances involved in security, user-controls, and versioning code inside Lambda. You will be guided via hands-on tutorials and lessons for understanding and learning to use AWS Lambda. So, it is recommended that you follow along this chapter with a laptop and an AWS account setup to easily execute the given instructions.

This chapter will cover the following topics:

- Triggers in AWS Lambda
- Lambda functions
- Functions as containers
- Configuring functions
- Testing Lambda functions
- Versioning Lambda functions
- Creating deployment packages

Triggers in AWS Lambda

Serverless functions are on-demand computational concepts. So, there has to be an event that needs to trigger a Lambda function so that the entire computational process is started. AWS Lambda has several events which can act as a trigger. Almost all services of AWS can act as AWS Lambda's triggers. Here is the list of services that you can use for generating events for Lambda to respond to:

- API Gateway
- AWS IoT
- CloudWatch Events
- CloudWatch Logs
- CodeCommit
- Cognito Sync Trigger
- DynamoDB
- Kinesis
- S3
- SNS

The triggers page of AWS Lambda looks like this:

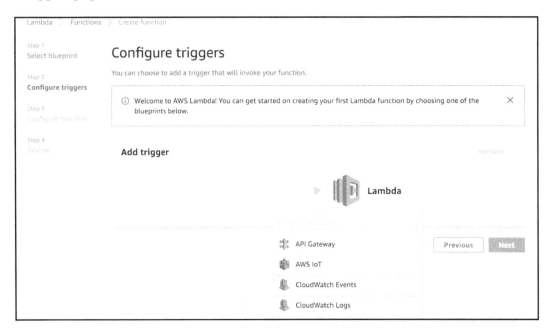

Let's take a look at some of the following important and widely-used triggers that are available, and understand how they can be leveraged as FaaS in the serverless paradigm. They are as follows:

- **API Gateway**: This trigger can be used to create efficient, scalable, and serverless APIs. One scenario where a serverless API makes sense would be while building a querying interface for S3. Let us assume that we have a bunch of text files in an S3 bucket. Whenever a user hits the API with a query parameter, which can be some word that we want to search in the text files in the bucket, the API Gateway's trigger will launch a Lambda function that executes the computational logic and workload for executing the query. The Lambda function that we want our API to trigger can be specified at the API creation time. The trigger will be created accordingly in the corresponding Lambda function's console. This is what it looks like:

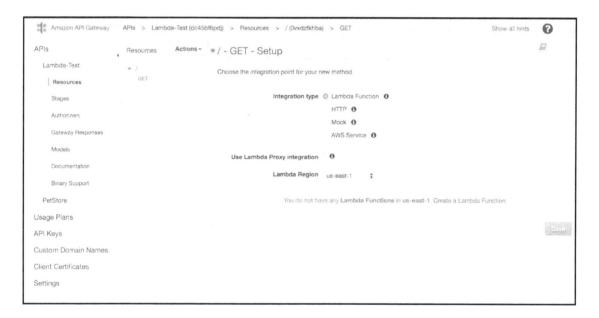

- **CloudWatch**: It events mostly help the user in setting the cron scheduling for Lambda. The CloudWatch Logs trigger is useful whenever a user wants to execute a computational workload depending on some keyword in the Cloudwatch Logs. However, the CloudWatch Alarms cannot trigger Lambda directly via the CloudWatch trigger. They have to be sent via a notification system, such as the **AWS Simple Notification Service** (**AWS SNS**). This is how you can create a cron execution in AWS Lambda. In the following screenshot, the Lambda function is set to execute every minute:

- **S3**: This is a document store of AWS. So, whenever a file is added, removed, or changed, an event will be sent to AWS Lambda when added as a trigger. So, if you want to do some computational workload on a file as soon as the file gets uploaded, then this trigger helps to do that. This is what an S3's event structure looks like:

```
{
    "Records":[
        {
            "eventVersion":"2.0",
            "eventSource":"aws:s3",
            "awsRegion":"us-east-1",
            "eventTime":The time, in ISO-8601 format, for example, 1970-01-01T00:00:00.000Z, when S3 fini.
            "eventName":"event-type",
            "userIdentity":{
                "principalId":"Amazon-customer-ID-of-the-user-who-caused-the-event"
            },
            "requestParameters":{
                "sourceIPAddress":"ip-address-where-request-came-from"
            },
            "responseElements":{
                "x-amz-request-id":"Amazon S3 generated request ID",
                "x-amz-id-2":"Amazon S3 host that processed the request"
            },
            "s3":{
                "s3SchemaVersion":"1.0",
                "configurationId":"ID found in the bucket notification configuration",
                "bucket":{
                    "name":"bucket-name",
                    "ownerIdentity":{
                        "principalId":"Amazon-customer-ID-of-the-bucket-owner"
                    },
                    "arn":"bucket-ARN"
                },
                "object":{
                    "key":"object-key",
                    "size":object-size,
                    "eTag":"object eTag",
                    "versionId":"object version if bucket is versioning-enabled, otherwise null",
                    "sequencer": "a string representation of a hexadecimal value used to determine event se
                        only used with PUTs and DELETEs"
                }
            }
        },
```

- **AWS SNS**: The SNS service of AWS helps users to send notifications to other systems. This service can also be used for catching CloudWatch Alarms and sending the notifications to a Lambda function for computational execution. This is what a sample SNS event looks like:

Amazon SNS Sample Event

⧉ Copy

```
{
  "Records": [
    {
      "EventVersion": "1.0",
      "EventSubscriptionArn": eventsubscriptionarn,
      "EventSource": "aws:sns",
      "Sns": {
        "SignatureVersion": "1",
        "Timestamp": "1970-01-01T00:00:00.000Z",
        "Signature": "EXAMPLE",
        "SigningCertUrl": "EXAMPLE",
        "MessageId": "95df01b4-ee98-5cb9-9903-4c221d41eb5e",
        "Message": "Hello from SNS!",
        "MessageAttributes": {
          "Test": {
            "Type": "String",
            "Value": "TestString"
          },
          "TestBinary": {
            "Type": "Binary",
            "Value": "TestBinary"
          }
        },
        "Type": "Notification",
        "UnsubscribeUrl": "EXAMPLE",
        "TopicArn": topicarn,
        "Subject": "TestInvoke"
      }
    }
  ]
}
```

Lambda functions

Lambda functions are the core operating parts of a serverless architecture. They contain the code which is supposed to be executed. These functions are executed whenever the trigger attached to it has been set off. We have already learned about some of the most popular Lambda triggers in the previous section.

Whenever a Lambda function is triggered, it creates a container with the respective settings set by the user. We'll learn more about the container in our next section.

The spinning up of containers takes a bit of time, which may result in a latency whenever a fresh invocation of a Lambda function is done, as it takes time to set up the environment and bootstrap the settings mentioned by the user in the **Advanced settings** tab. So, to overcome this latency, AWS thaws a container for some time for reuse in case of another Lambda invocation within the thawing time. So, using a thawed or a ready-made Lambda function helps in overcoming the latency problem. However, the same global namespace of the thawed container would be reused for the new invocation too.

So, if the Lambda function has any global variables that get manipulated inside the function, it is a good idea to convert them into local namespaces, as the manipulated global namespace variables will be reused, leading to faulty execution results of the Lambda function.

The user needs to specify the technical details for the Lambda function in the **Advanced Settings** tab, which include the following:

- **Memory (MB)**: This is the maximum memory that the Lambda function needs to be allocated for the purpose of your function. The CPU of the container would be assigned accordingly.
- **Timeout**: The maximum amount of time the function needs to execute before the container gets automatically stopped.
- **DLQ Resource**: This is a dead-letter setting to AWS Lambda. The user can add either an SQS queue or an SNS topic for configuring this. Lambda functions get asynchronously retried for at least five times on failure.
- **VPC**: This enables the Lambda function to access components or services in some particular VPCs. The Lambda function executes in a default VPC of its own.
- **KMS key**: If there are any environment variables entered along with the Lambda function, this helps us encrypt them using an **AWS Key Management Service (KMS)** by default.

The Lambda function's **Advanced settings** page looks like this:

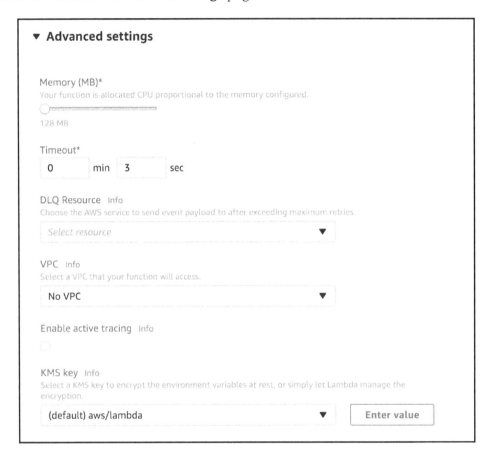

Functions as containers

For understanding the concept of functions being executed as/inside containers, we need to properly understand the concept of containers. To cite the definition of a container from the Docker documentation (`https://www.docker.com/what-docker`):

> *A container image is a lightweight, stand-alone, executable package of a piece of software*
> *that includes everything needed to run it: code, runtime, system tools, system libraries,*
> *settings.*

What is available for both Linux and Windows based applications; containerized software will always run the same, regardless of the environment.

Containers isolate software from its surroundings (for example, differences between development and staging environments) and help reduce conflicts between teams running different software on the same infrastructure.

So, the concept of containers is that they are self-sustainable isolated environments just like the containers in a container ship that can be hosted and be worked upon any host OS, the host OS being the host ship in our analogy. The figurative depiction of the analogy would look something like this:

Similar to the aforementioned analogy, AWS Lambda's functions are also launched inside a unique container for each function. So, let us understand this topic in more detail, point by point:

1. The Lambda function can be in the form of a single code file or in the form of a **deployment package**. The deployment package is a zipped file that includes the core function file along with the libraries which would be used by the function. We shall be learning in detail about how to create the deployment package in the *Creating deployment packages* section of this chapter.

2. Whenever a function is triggered or started, AWS spins up an EC2 instance with the AWS Linux operating system for running the function. The configuration of the instance would be dependent on the ones provided by the user in the **Advanced settings** tab of the Lambda function.

3. There is a maximum time limit of 300 seconds, or 5 minutes, for a function to execute successfully, after which the container would be destroyed. So, this needs to be kept in mind while designing the Lambda functions and/or the deployment packages.

Configuring functions

In this section, we will go through the ways of configuring Lambda functions and understand all the settings in great detail. Like in the previous section, we will learn about each configuration and its settings, as follows:

1. You can go to the page of AWS Lambda by selecting it from the drop-down menu that is present in the top-left corner of the AWS console. This can be done as follows:

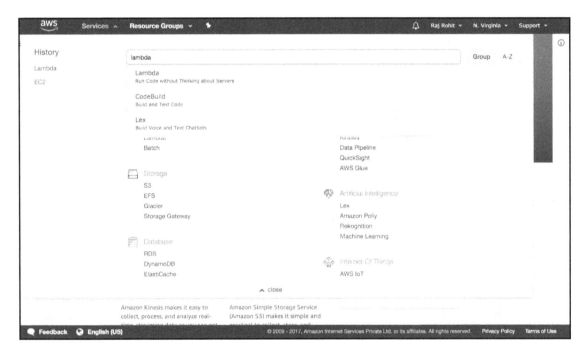

2. Once the **Lambda** option is selected, it redirects the user to the **AWS Lambda** console, which looks something like this:

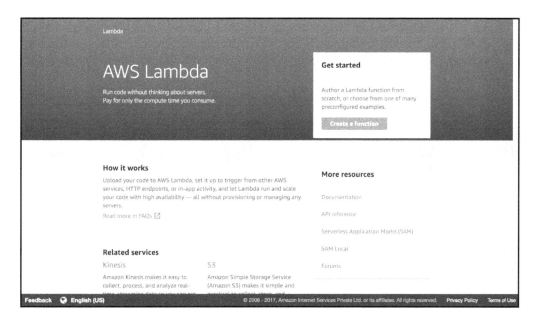

3. For creating a function, you need to click on the orange **Create a function** button on the right. This will open a console for the function creation. This looks something like this:

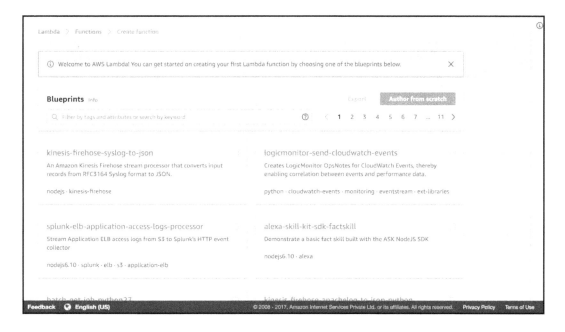

4. Let's create a function from scratch in order to understand the configurations better. So, for doing that, click on the **Author from scratch** button on the top-right corner. After clicking it, the user will be directed to Lambda's first-run console, which looks something like this:

5. This page has three configurations which the user can select, which are **Name**, **Role**, and **Existing role**. The **Name** value is where the user can enter the name of the Lambda function. The **Role** value is how you can define permissions in the AWS environment. The **Role** value's drop-down list would contain the following options: **Choose an existing role**, **Create new role from template(s)**, and **Create a custom role**. They can be seen as follows:

The **Choose an existing role** option will enable us to select an already existing role with pre-configured permissions. The second option helps the user with creating a role from pre-baked templates. The **Create a custom role** option allows the user to create a role with permissions from scratch. The list of pre-baked roles looks like this:

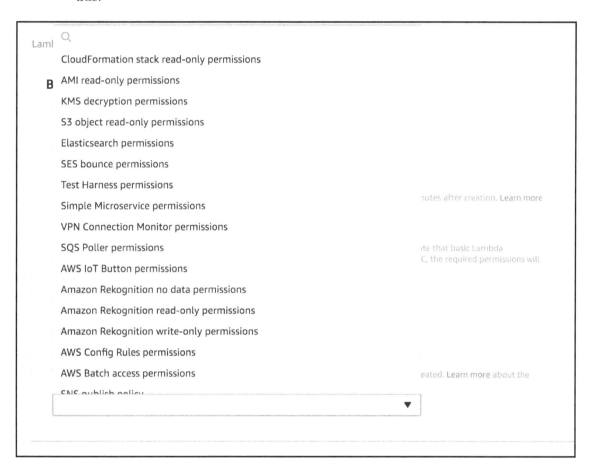

6. Select one from the pre-baked templates for the sake of this tutorial. By pressing **Create function** in the lower-right part of the screen, we will land on the Lambda function's creation page, which looks similar to this:

7. The preceding page indicates that we have successfully created an AWS Lambda function. We shall now explore the advanced settings of this function. They are present in the lower part of the same console. They will look something like this:

We shall now try to understand each of those parts in detail.

8. The unfurled **Environment variables** section contains text boxes to enter the key-value pair of environment variables that will be used by our function. One can also optionally mention details on the encryption setting that we want to have for the environment variables. The encryption needs to be done via **AWS KMS** (**Key Management Service**). The unfurled settings box of the environment variables looks something like this:

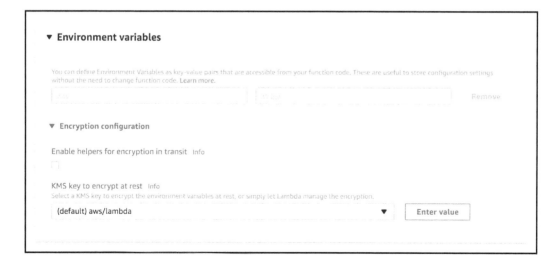

9. The next settings section is **Tags**. This is similar to the tagging feature of all the available AWS services for easy service discovery purposes. So, similar to all AWS services's tags, this also needs just a key and a value. The unfurled **Tags** section looks something like this:

10. The next section that will be visible after the **Tags** section is the **Execution role** section, in which the user can set the **Identity Access Management (IAM)** role for the execution of the Lambda function. As we have already discussed what IAM roles are previously in the book, we will not be covering that again here. If the user has not set the role when creating the function itself, they can always set that here. The section will be visible in the Lambda console as follows:

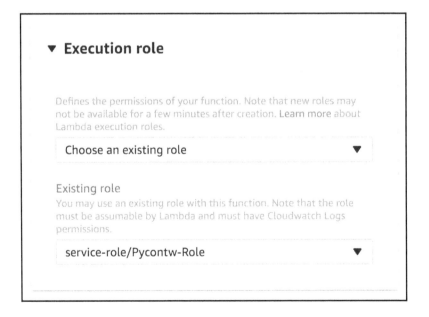

11. The next section is the **Basic settings** section, which includes settings such as the memory of the Lambda container, time-out for the container, and the description for the Lambda function. The memory of the container can range from 128 MB to 1,536 MB. The user can choose any value within that range and will be billed accordingly. The time-out can be set from 1 second to 300 seconds, which is 5 minutes. The time-out is the time which the Lambda function and its container would run before being stopped or terminated. The next setting is the **Description** value of the Lambda function, which acts as the metadata of a Lambda function. The section looks like this in the console:

12. The next section is the **Network** section, which is also about the network settings of the Lambda function related to **AWS's Virtual Private Cloud** (**VPC**) and related subnets. Even if **No VPC** is selected as an option, AWS Lambda runs in its own secure VPC. However, if your Lambda function accesses or deals with any other service which is in a particular VPC or in a subnet, the corresponding information needs to be added in this section so that the network allows traffic from the Lambda function's container. This section looks like this in the console:

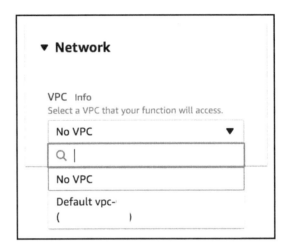

The sensitive information in the preceding screenshot, such as the IP address and the ID of the VPC, are masked for security purposes.

13. The next section is the **Debugging and error handling** section. This section enables the user to set up measures for ensuring fault tolerance and exception handling of the Lambda function. This includes the **Dead Letter Queue** (**DLQ**) settings.

14. Lambda automatically retries failed executions for asynchronous invocations. So, the payloads that were not processed would be automatically forwarded to the DLQ resource. The DLQ settings look like this in the Lambda console:

The user can also enable active tracing for the Lambda functions, which would help in detailed monitoring of the Lambda container. This setting in the **Debugging and error handling** section of the Lambda console looks like this:

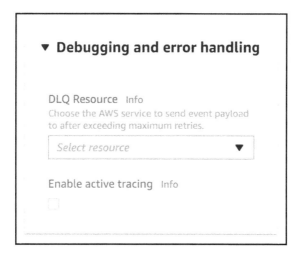

Testing Lambda functions

Just like every other software system and programming paradigm, proper testing of Lambda functions and serverless architectures is very important before deploying into production. We will try to understand the testing of Lambda functions in the following points:

1. In the top-most bar of the Lambda console, one can observe the **Save and test** option, which is represented by an orange button. This button saves the Lambda function and then runs the configured tests on that function. This looks something like this in the console:

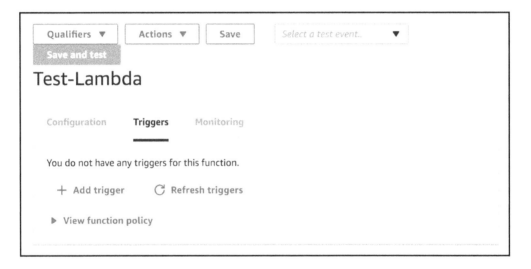

2. Also, in the same bar, there exists a drop-down menu that reads **Select a test event...**. This contains a list of testing events available for testing Lambda functions. The drop-down looks like this:

3. Now, for further configuration of test events for the Lambda function, the user needs to select the **Configure test events** option in the drop-down. This will open a popup with the test events menu, which looks like this:

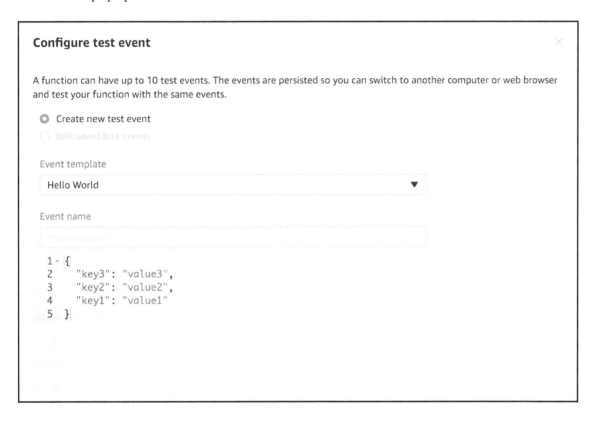

Configure test event

A function can have up to 10 test events. The events are persisted so you can switch to another computer or web browser and test your function with the same events.

○ Create new test event

○ Edit saved test events

Event template

Hello World ▼

Event name

```
1 ▾ {
2     "key3": "value3",
3     "key2": "value2",
4     "key1": "value1"
5 }
```

4. That would open the basic **Hello World** template, which has three pre-configured JSON format test events, or edge cases. However, depending on what the Lambda function does, one can select some other test event. The available list of testing templates can be seen in the **Event template** drop-down menu. The list in the drop-down looks something like this:

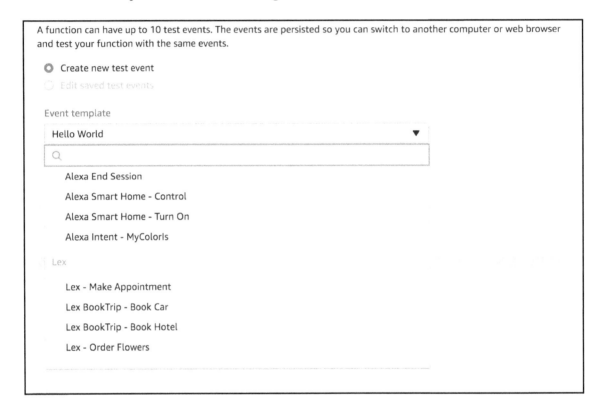

5. For example, let's imagine we are building a pipeline that involves the Lambda function getting started whenever an image file is added to an S3 bucket, and the function does some image processing tasks and puts it back to some data store. The test event of the **S3 Put** notification looks something like this:

Event template

S3 Put ▼

Event name

```
 1 ▾ {
 2 ▾   "Records": [
 3 ▾     {
 4         "eventVersion": "2.0",
 5         "eventTime": "1970-01-01T00:00:00.000Z",
 6 ▾       "requestParameters": {
 7           "sourceIPAddress": "127.0.0.1"
 8         },
 9 ▾       "s3": {
10           "configurationId": "testConfigRule",
11 ▾         "object": {
12             "eTag": "0123456789abcdef0123456789abcdef",
13             "sequencer": "0A1B2C3D4E5F678901",
14             "key": "HappyFace.jpg",
15             "size": 1024
16           },
17 ▾         "bucket": {
18             "arn": "arn:aws:s3:::mybucket",
19             "name": "sourcebucket",
20 ▾           "ownerIdentity": {
21               "principalId": "EXAMPLE"
22             }
23           },
24           "s3SchemaVersion": "1.0"
25         },
26 ▾       "responseElements": {
```

Cancel   Create

6. After selecting or creating a test event, the user can select the **Create** option in the
    bottom-right corner of the event creation console, wherein you shall be asked to
    enter a name for the event. After entering the necessary details, the user will be
    re-directed back to the Lambda console. Now, when you check the
    TestEvent drop-down in the Lambda console, you can see the saved test event in
    the list. This can be verified as follows:

| Qualifiers ▼ | Actions ▼ | Save | TestEvent ▼ |

Save and test

Saved Test Events

Test-Lambda

TestEvent

Configure test events

Configuration   **Triggers**   Monitoring

You do not have any triggers for this function.

As I have named the event as **TestEvent**, the test is visible by the same name in the events drop-down menu.

6. Additionally, when we take a closer look at the event structure of S3 in the test event, we can observe the meta-details that are being made available to the Lambda function. The event structure looks like this:

```
{
    "Records":[
        {
            "eventVersion":"2.0",
            "eventSource":"aws:s3",
            "awsRegion":"us-west-2",
            "eventTime":"1970-01-01T00:00:00.000Z",
            "eventName":"ObjectCreated:Put",
            "userIdentity":{
                "principalId":"AIDAJDPLRKLG7UEXAMPLE"
            },
            "requestParameters":{
                "sourceIPAddress":"127.0.0.1"
            },
            "responseElements":{
                "x-amz-request-id":"C3D13FE58DE4C810",
                "x-amz-id-2":"FMyUVURIY8/IgAtTv8xRjskZQpcIZ9KG4V5Wp6S7S/JRWeUWerMUE5JgHvANOjpD"
            },
            "s3":{
                "s3SchemaVersion":"1.0",
                "configurationId":"testConfigRule",
                "bucket":{
                    "name":"sourcebucket",
                    "ownerIdentity":{
                        "principalId":"A3NL1KOZZKExample"
                    },
                    "arn":"arn:aws:s3:::sourcebucket"
                },
                "object":{
                    "key":"HappyFace.jpg",
                    "size":1024,
                    "eTag":"d41d8cd98f00b204e9800998ecf8427e",
                    "versionId":"096fKKXTRTtl3on89fVO.nfljtsv6qko"
                }
            }
        }
    ]
}
```

Versioning Lambda functions

The concept of the **Version Control System** (**VCS**) is for controlling and managing versions of code. This functionality is available directly from the main Lambda console. Let's try and learn how to version our Lambda functions:

1. The first option in the **Actions** drop-down in the Lambda console is the **Publish new version** option. This option can be seen here:

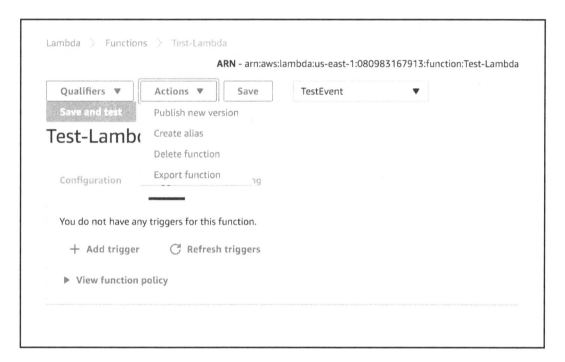

2. When the **Publish new version** option is selected, the versioning popup of the Lambda console would be seen on the console. This would ask about the name for the new version of your Lambda function. The popup looks something like this:

Publish new version from $LATEST

          ×

Publishing a new version will save a "snapshot" of the code and configuration of the $LATEST version. You will be unable to edit the new version's code. Please click to confirm.

Version description

Cancel   Publish

3. After clicking the **Publish** button, you will be re-directed to the main Lambda console. The successfully created Lambda version in the console looks something like this:

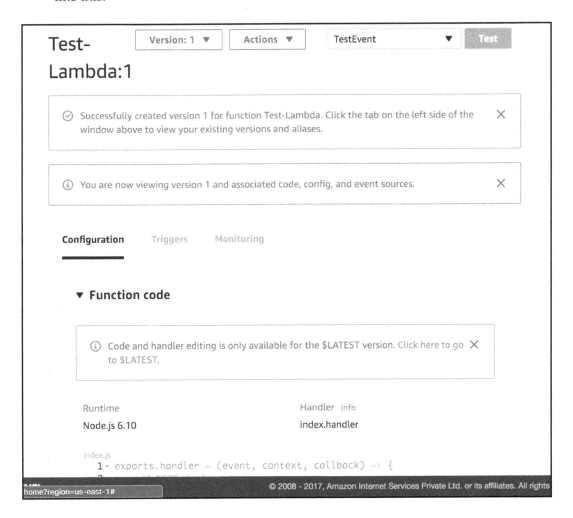

4. In the bottom half of the page, the following message can be noticed: **Code and handler editing is only available for the $LATEST version**. This means that one can only edit the code in the version named **$LATEST**. The versioned version of Lambda functions are read-only and cannot be edited and manipulated. When something goes wrong or when the user wants to revert back or refer to a previous version, that version will overlay the **$LATEST** version to make edits possible. The message looks like this:

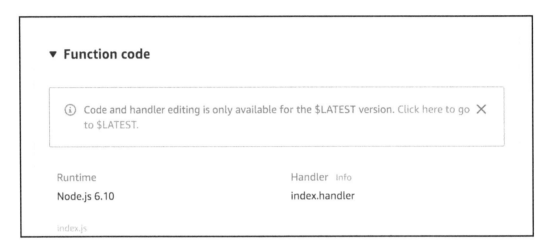

5. When the **Click here to go to $LATEST** link is clicked, the user will be re-directed to the **$LATEST** version of the function, which can be edited and manipulated by the user. The console of the **$LATEST** version of the Lambda function looks like this:

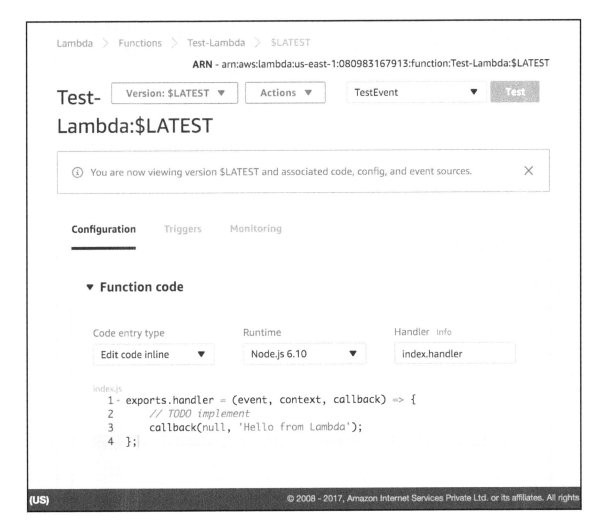

Creating deployment packages

Lambda functions that have external libraries as dependencies can be packaged as deployment packages and be uploaded into the AWS Lambda console. This is very similar to creating a virtual environment in Python. So in this section, we shall learn and understand the process of creating Python deployment for using in the Lambda functions. We shall try and understand the process of creating deployment packages in detail, as follows:

1. Deployment packages are generally in the format of ZIP packages. The contents of the ZIP package is exactly the same as a normal library of any programming language.

2. The package structure should be such that the library folders and the function file are in the same destination or in the same hierarchy inside the folder structure of the deployment package. The layout looks something like this:

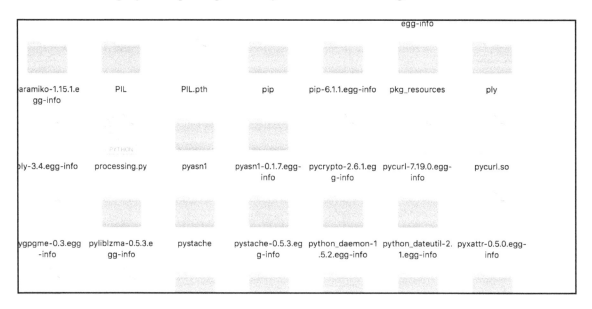

3. The Python libraries can be installed by using the `pip install <library_name> -t <path_of_the_target_folder>` command. This will install the package inside the target folder. This can be done as in the following screenshot:

```
+  ServerlessBook sudo pip install numpy -t TestDir
Password:
The directory '/Users/Dawny33/Library/Caches/pip/http' or its parent directory is not owned by the current user and the cache has been disabled. Please check
the permissions and owner of that directory. If executing pip with sudo, you may want sudo's -H flag.
The directory '/Users/Dawny33/Library/Caches/pip' or its parent directory is not owned by the current user and caching wheels has been disabled. check the per
missions and owner of that directory. If executing pip with sudo, you may want sudo's -H flag.
Collecting numpy
  Downloading numpy-1.13.3-cp27-cp27m-macosx_10_6_intel.macosx_10_9_intel.macosx_10_9_x86_64.macosx_10_10_intel.macosx_10_10_x86_64.whl (4.6MB)
    100% |                                | 4.6MB 172kB/s
Installing collected packages: numpy
Successfully installed numpy-1.13.3
```

4. Now, when we have the entire deployment package's folder along with the library folders ready, we need to zip all of the folders including the Lambda function file before uploading it into the console. The following screenshot shows how the zipping needs to be done as per the folder hierarchy:

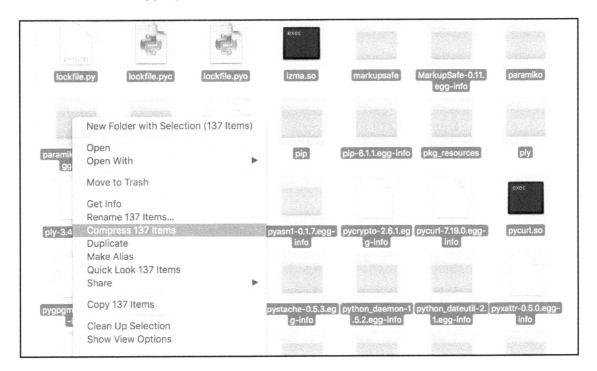

5. Now, as the zipped package is ready, we shall be trying to upload the package to the Lambda console for processing. For uploading a Lambda package, we need to select the drop-down list of the **Code entry type** option in the console. The selection looks like this in the Lambda console:

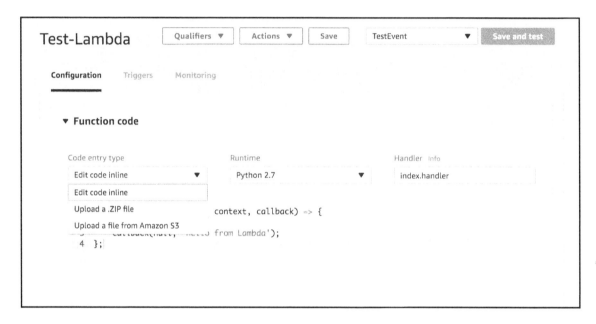

6. Once the **Upload a .ZIP file** option is selected, the uploader will become visible, where the user can directly upload the deployment package or even upload it via an S3 bucket. The wizard would look like this in the Lambda console:

7. As mentioned previously, the user can choose to upload the deployment package via an S3 file location too. This wizard looks like this in the Lambda console:

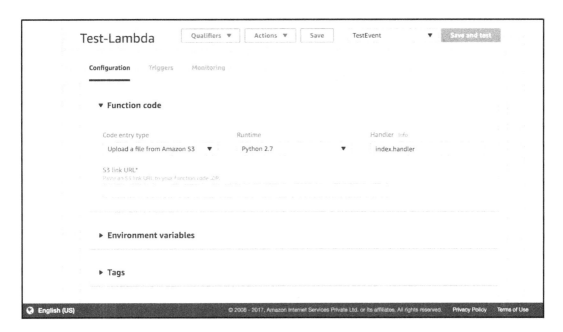

8. The deployment package's naming should be aligned with the values entered in the handler part of the settings. The deployment package's name and the Lambda function file's name are separated by a dot (.) and arranged in that order. This can be explicitly seen in the following screenshot:

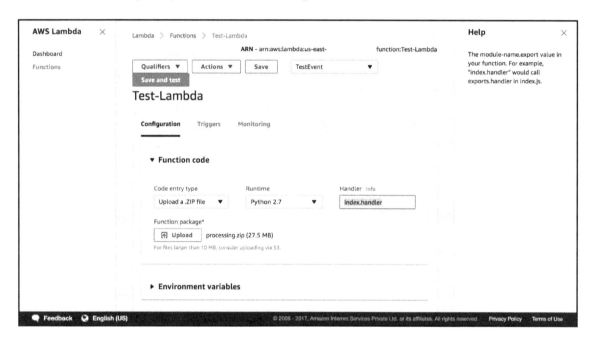

index should be the name of the Lambda function's file name deployment package. The handler function file is the name of the core function handler inside, which is the Lambda function. As AWS's documentation states:

The module-name export value in your function". For example, index.handler would call exports.handler in index.py.

Summary

In this chapter, we have learned the concepts of how triggers work for AWS Lambda and how to select triggers depending on the problem statement and time intervals, in case of cron job triggers. We understood what Lambda functions are, along with understanding their functionalities and settings related to memory, VPCs, security, and fault tolerance. We also learned about the way container reuse is done under the hood specifically for AWS Lambda. Then, we covered event-driven functions and how they are implemented under the hood, the concept of containers, and their uses and applications in the domain of software engineering in general. Most importantly, from the concepts we learned regarding containers, we can now appreciate the options for choosing containers for running the Lambda functions.

After that, we talked about all the configuration settings available in the AWS Lambda dashboard, which are necessary to build and run a Lambda function from start to finish without any settings-related problems. We also learned about and understood the security settings inside Lambda so that the necessary VPC details and security keys settings are taken care of when configuring our Lambda functions. This was followed by testing Lambda functions depending on the choice of trigger selected. We learned what the responses of various AWS services look like, as they are the inputs for the Lambda functions. We then learned how to write custom hand-made tests for custom testing purposes.

Following that, we saw how versioning happens for the AWS Lambda functions. We learned the differences between past and present versions. We also learned that the present version is immutable, unlike the past versions, and also how to revert to past versions without much effort. We also learned how to create deployment packages for functions that have dependencies on external packages, which are not included in Python's standard library. We came across the function code naming nuances, including the filename and the method handler names, followed by the two ways deployment packages can be uploaded to the Lambda console; one being a manual upload and the other being from an S3 file location.

In the next chapter, we will be gaining a detailed understanding of the different triggers available in the Lambda console and how to use them. We will also learn about implementing them in Python code. We will understand the event structures and the responses from different AWS services and use that to build our Lambda functions. We will understand how to integrate each trigger into a Lambda function and do a specific task in Python. Finally, we will also be learning about ideas and best practices on how to move your existing infrastructures to serverless using the serverless paradigm.

Setting Up Serverless Architectures

3

So far, we have understood what the serverless paradigm is, and also how serverless systems work. We have also understood how AWS Lambda's serverless tool works. We have also learned the basics of how triggers work in AWS Lambda as well as a detailed understanding of the system settings and configuration available to the user in the Lambda environment. We have also learned how the Lambda console works, and also how to identify and use various parts of the Lambda console in detail, including code deployment, trigger manipulation, deploying tests in the console, versioning our Lambda function, and also the different settings available.

By the end of this chapter, you will have a clear understanding of all the important triggers available for AWS Lambda and how you can use them to set up efficient Lambda architectures. You will also understand what an event structure is, and what an event structure looks like for some AWS resources, and how you can use that knowledge to write and deploy better trigger-based Lambda architectures.

This chapter will cover the following points:

- S3 trigger
- SNS trigger
- SQS trigger
- CloudWatch Event and Logs trigger

S3 trigger

S3 is the AWS object storage service, where the user can store and retrieve any type of object. In this section, we shall be learning how the S3 trigger works, what the event structure of an S3 event looks like, and also how to make use of them in the learning to build a Lambda function.

We will be building a Lambda function that does the following:

1. Receives a PUT request event from the S3 service
2. Prints the name of the file and other major details
3. Transfers that file to a different bucket

So, let's get started on learning how to use the S3 trigger efficiently. We will be working on this task step-by-step, as follows:

1. Firstly, we need to create two S3 buckets for the task. One will be the bucket where the file will be uploaded by the user. The other will be the one where the file is transferred and uploaded by the Lambda function.
2. The S3 console looks like the following screenshot when there are no pre-existing buckets. You can go there by selecting the **S3** service from the drop-down **Services** menu in the top-left of your AWS console:

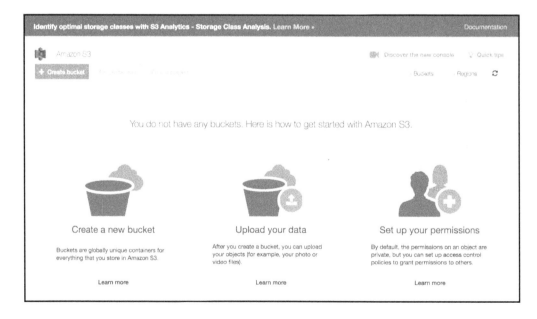

3. Let's create two buckets, namely `receiver-bucket` and `sender-bucket`.

4. The `sender-bucket` bucket will be used as the bucket where the user uploads the files. The `receiver-bucket` bucket is the one where the Lambda function uploads the files. So, as per our problem statement, whenever we upload files to the `sender-bucket` bucket, the Lambda function gets triggered and the files get uploaded to `receiver-bucket`.

5. When we click on the **Create bucket** button in the S3 console, we get a dialog that looks like this:

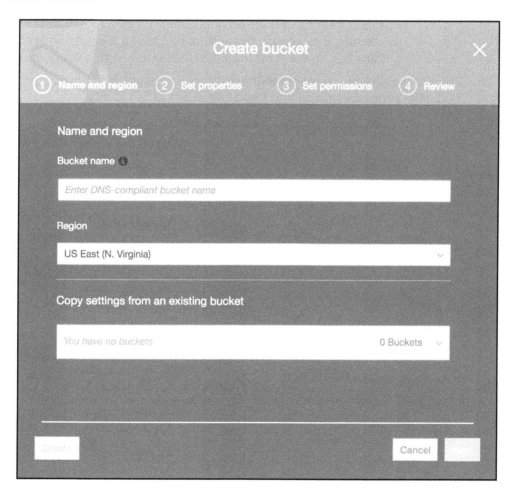

6. In the preceding dialog, we need to enter the following settings:
    - **Bucket Name**: As the name suggests, we need to enter the name of the bucket we are creating. For the creation of the first bucket, name it `sender-bucket` and name the second bucket `receiver-bucket`.
    - **Region**: This is an AWS region we want the bucket to reside in. You can use the default region for this or the region closest to wherever you are located.
    - **Copy settings from an existing bucket**: This specifies whether we want to use the same settings as in some other bucket in the console for this bucket too. As we do not currently have any other bucket in our console, we can skip this setting by leaving it empty. After this, you can click on the **Next** button in the bottom-right part of the popup.

7. Once we click **Next**, we get redirected to the second tab of the popup, which is the **Set properties** menu and looks like this:

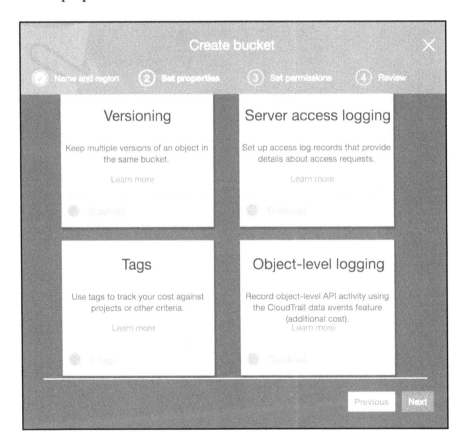

8. In this part of the popup, we need to decide on the following settings:

- **Versioning**: This is relevant if we want to keep multiple versions of the files in the S3 bucket. This setting is required when you need a Git style versioning for your S3 bucket. Note that the storage cost would be included in line with the number of versioned documents.
- **Server access logging**: This will log all the access requests to the S3 bucket. This helps debug any security breaches and secure the S3 bucket and the files.
- **Tags**: This will tag the bucket using a *Name:Value* style, the same style of tagging as we learned for Lambda functions.
- **Object-level logging**: This will use the CloudTrail service of AWS to log all the access requests and other details and activities on the S3 bucket. This will also include CloudTrail costs too. So, use this feature only if you need detailed logging. We shall skip using this for this section.

9. After finishing creating the buckets, the S3 console will look like this, with both the created buckets listed:

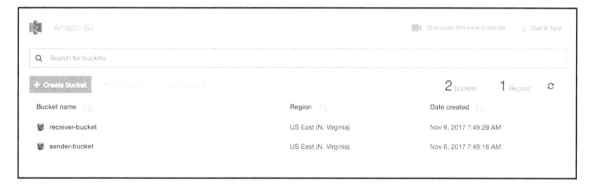

10. We have successfully created S3 buckets for our task. Now, we have to create a Lambda function that can recognize an object upload in the `sender-bucket` bucket and send that file to the `receiver-bucket` bucket.

11. While creating the Lambda function, this time choose the **s3-get-object-python** blueprint from the listed options available:

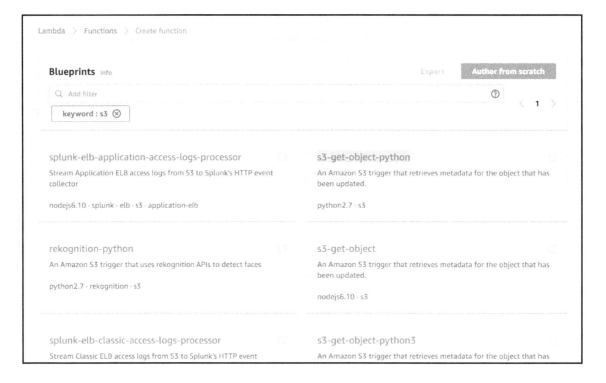

12. Configure the bucket details in the next step. In the **Bucket** section, select the **sender-bucket** bucket and select the **Object Created (All)** option in the **Event type** action. This is because we want to send a notification to Lambda whenever an object gets created in the `sender-bucket` bucket. The completed part of the section will look like this:

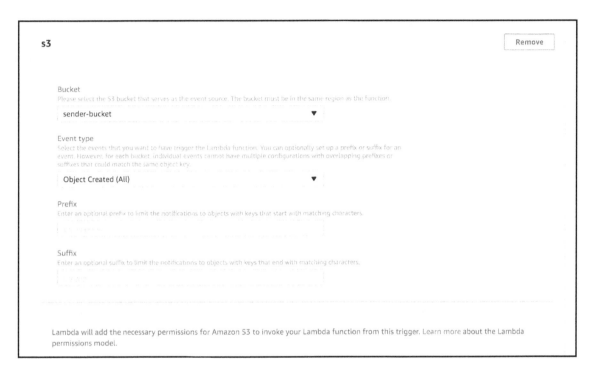

13. Once you have enabled the trigger, Lambda helps you by creating a boilerplate code for the task. All we need to do is write the code to put the object into the `receiver-bucket` bucket. The boilerplate code can be seen in the **Lambda function code** section:

Lambda function code

Code is pre-configured by the chosen blueprint. You can configure it after you create the function.

Runtime
Python 2.7

```
 1  from __future__ import print_function
 2
 3  import json
 4  import urllib
 5  import boto3
 6
 7  print('Loading function')
 8
 9  s3 = boto3.client('s3')
10
11
12  def lambda_handler(event, context):
13      #print("Received event: " + json.dumps(event, indent=2))
14
15      # Get the object from the event and show its content type
16      bucket = event['Records'][0]['s3']['bucket']['name']
17      key = urllib.unquote_plus(event['Records'][0]['s3']['object']['key'].encode('utf8'))
18      try:
19          response = s3.get_object(Bucket=bucket, Key=key)
20          print('CONTENT TYPE: ' + response['ContentType'])
21          return response['ContentType']
22      except Exception as e:
23          print(e)
24          print('Error getting object {} from bucket {}. Make sure they exist and your bucket is in the
25          raise e
26
```

14. When this step has been completed and you have clicked the **Create function** button, you can see the **Triggers** section of the Lambda console, which displays a success message in green at the top:

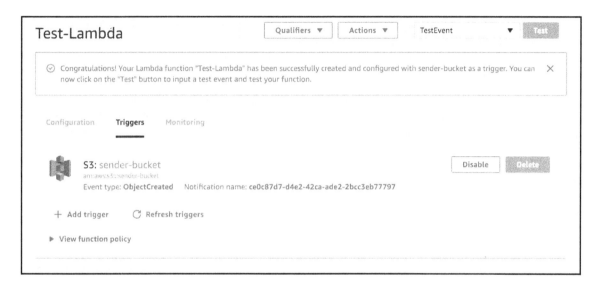

15. I have uploaded a small image file into the sender-bucket bucket. So, now the contents of the **sender-bucket** bucket look like this:

16. As soon as this file had been uploaded, the Lambda function got triggered. The Lambda function code looks like this:

```
from __future__ import print_function

import json
import urllib
import boto3
from botocore.client import Config

print('Loading function')
sts_client = boto3.client('sts', use_ssl=True)

# Assume a Role for temporary credentials
assumedRoleObject = sts_client.assume_role(
RoleArn="arn:aws:iam::080983167913:role/service-role/Pycontw-
Role",
RoleSessionName="AssumeRoleSession1"
)
credentials = assumedRoleObject['Credentials']
region = 'us-east-1'

def lambda_handler(event, context):
    #print("Received event: " + json.dumps(event, indent=2))

    # Get the object from the event and show its content type
    bucket = event['Records'][0]['s3']['bucket']['name']
    key = urllib.unquote_plus(event['Records'][0]['s3']
['object']['key'].encode('utf8'))
    try:
        # Creates a session
        session = boto3.Session(credentials['AccessKeyId'],
credentials['SecretAccessKey'] ,
aws_session_token=credentials['SessionToken'],
region_name=region)

        #Instantiates an S3 resource
        s3 = session.resource('s3',
config=Config(signature_version='s3v4'), use_ssl=True)

        #Instantiates an S3 client
        client = session.client('s3',
config=Config(signature_version='s3v4'), use_ssl=True)

        # Gets the list of objects of a bucket
        response = client.list_objects(Bucket=bucket)
```

```
            destination_bucket = 'receiver-bucket'
            source_bucket = 'sender-bucket'

            # Adding all the file names in the S3 bucket in an
array
            keys = []
            if 'Contents' in response:
                for item in response['Contents']:
                    keys.append(item['Key']);

            # Add all the files in the bucket into the receiver
bucket
            for key in keys:
                path = source_bucket + '/' + key
                print(key)
            s3.Object(destination_bucket,
key).copy_from(CopySource=path)

        Exception as e:
            print(e)
print('Error getting object {} from bucket {}. Make sure they
exist and your bucket is in the same region as this
function.'.format(key, bucket))
raise e
```

17. Now, when you run the Lambda function, you can see the same file in the **receiver-bucket** bucket:

SNS trigger

The SNS notification service can be used across multiple use cases, one of which involves triggering Lambda functions. The SNS trigger is popularly used as an interface between the AWS CloudWatch service and Lambda.

So, in this section, we will do the following:

1. Create an SNS topic
2. Create a CloudWatch alarm for our `receiver-bucket` bucket to monitor the number of objects in the bucket
3. Once the objects count reaches 5, the alarm will be set to **ALERT** and the corresponding notification will be sent to the SNS topic that we have just created
4. This SNS topic will then trigger a Lambda function, which prints out a **Hello World** message for us

This will help you understand how to monitor different AWS services and set up alarms for some thresholds for those metrics. And depending on whether the service's metrics have hit that threshold or not, the Lambda function will get triggered.

The process flow for this is as follows:

1. SNS topics can be created from the SNS dashboard. By clicking on the **Create topic** option, you will be redirected to the topic creation dashboard of SNS. The SNS dashboard of AWS looks like this:

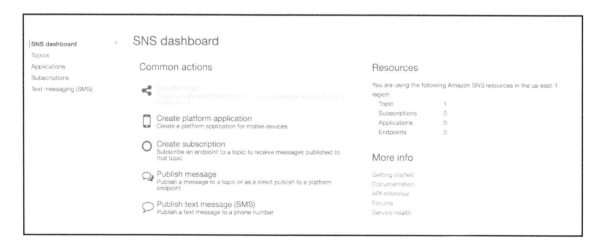

The SNS topic creation wizard in the next step looks like this:

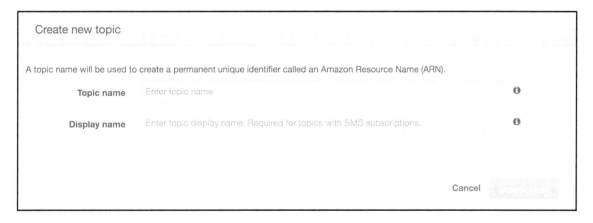

In this creation wizard, you can name the SNS topic that you are creating, and add any meta information you want to.

2. Once the topic is created, you can view it in the **Topics** menu, which is on the left of your SNS dashboard. The button looks like this:

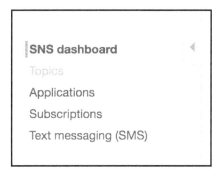

Upon clicking the **Topics** tab, a list of topics will be displayed, as shown in the following screenshot:

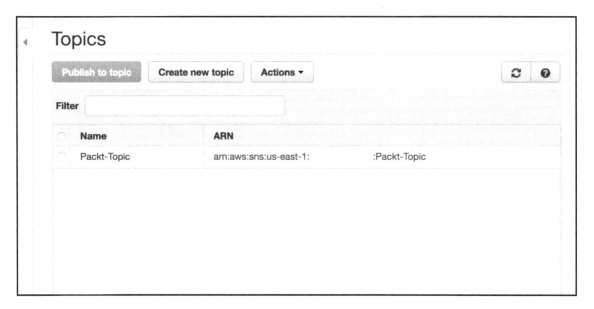

3. Now that we have successfully created an SNS topic, we shall create a CloudWatch alarm to monitor our S3 bucket for files. The AWS **CloudWatch** dashboard looks something like this:

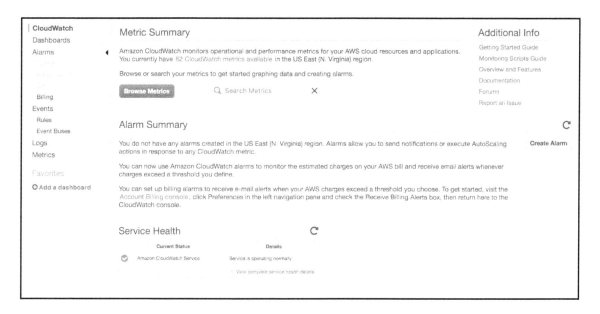

4. Now, we can go to the **Alarms** page by clicking the **Alarms** button in the list on the left of the dashboard. The AWS **Alarms** page of looks like this:

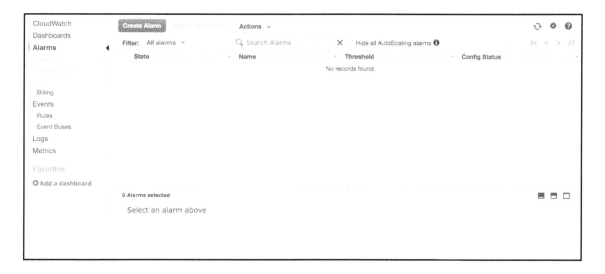

5. Next, click on **Create Alarm** to create an alarm. This will open an alarm creation wizard with multiple options. The wizard looks like this, depending on the services running in your AWS ecosystem:

6. As we intend to create an alarm for our S3 bucket, we can go to the **S3 Metrics** tab and ignore the rest of the available metrics. If you click on the **Storage Metrics** option in the **S3 Metrics** category, you will be re-directed to another alarm creation wizard that looks like the following, depending on the number of buckets you have in your S3:

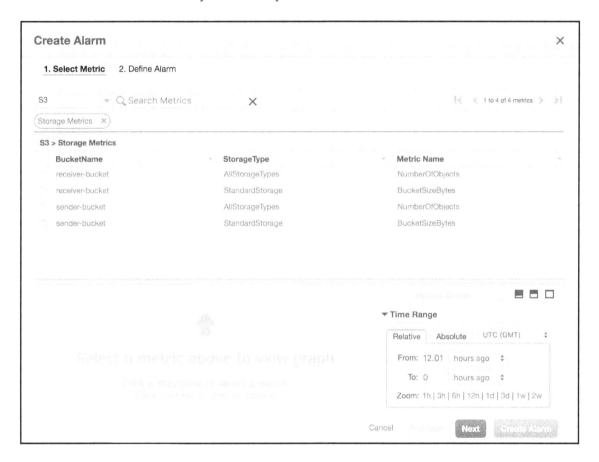

7. If you observe the options in the **Metric Name** column, you will see two options available for each bucket: **NumberOfObjects** and **BucketSizeBytes**. They are self-explanatory and we will only need the **NumberOfObjects** option for the `receiver-bucket` bucket. So, select that option and click **Next**:

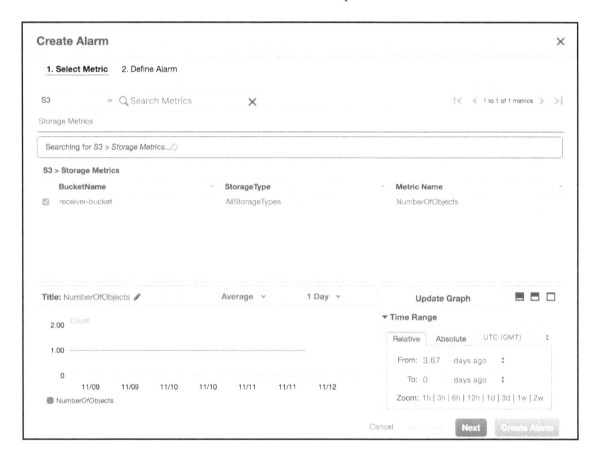

This will take you to the alarm definition wizard, where you need to specify the details of the SNS topic and the threshold for the alarm. The wizard looks like this:

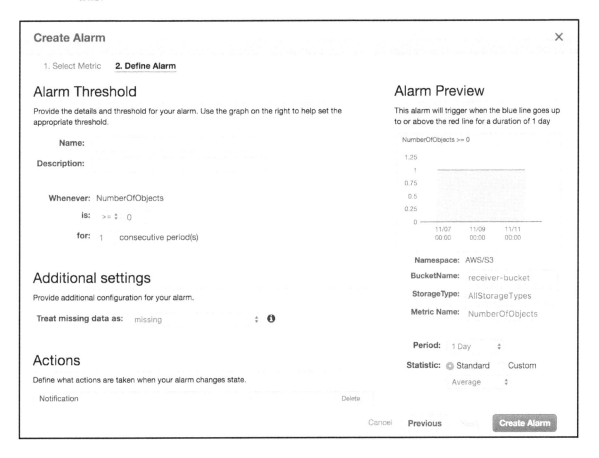

8. Add in the details for the threshold and the name of the alarm. The threshold is five files, which means that the alarm will be triggered as soon as the number of files in the corresponding bucket (`receiver-bucket` in our case) reaches a total of five. The wizard looks like this:

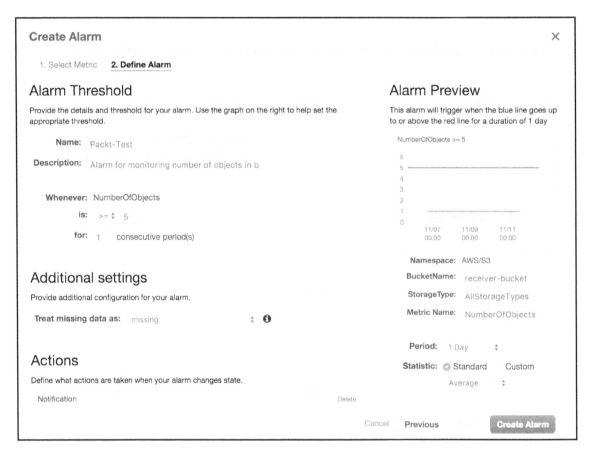

9. In the **Actions** option, we can configure the alarm to send the notification to the SNS topic that we have just created. You can select the topic from the drop-down list, as follows:

10. Once we have configured the SNS topic, we can click on the blue **Create Alarm** button at the bottom. This will create the alarm that is linked to the SNS topic as a notification pipeline. The created alarm will look like this on the dashboard:

11. Now, we can move on to building the Lambda function for the task. For this particular task, use the **sns-message-python** blueprint while creating our Lambda function:

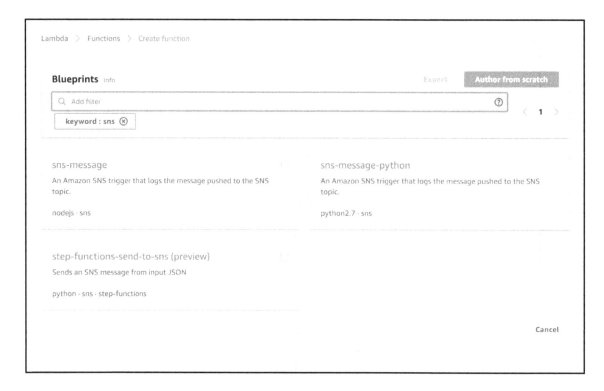

11. In the previous step, when you have selected the blueprint, you will be asked to enter some meta information regarding your Lambda function, just like we did previously while creating Lambda functions. In the same wizard, you will also be asked to mention the name of the SNS topic. You can specify it here:

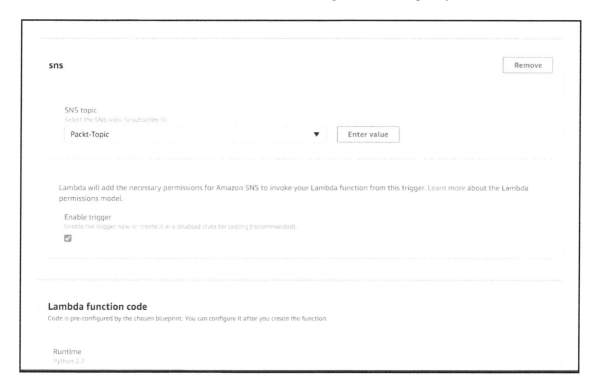

12. Now that we have selected all the options for the Lambda function correctly, we can now go on to the code. The desired code will look like this:

```
Code entry type                    Runtime                           Handler  Info

Edit code inline          ▼        Python 2.7              ▼         lambda_function.lambda_handler


lambda_function.py
  1  from __future__ import print_function
  2
  3  import json
  4
  5  print('Loading function')
  6
  7
  8 ·def lambda_handler(event, context):
  9      #print("Received event: " + json.dumps(event, indent=2))
 10      message = event['Records'][0]['Sns']['Message']
 11      print("From SNS: " + message)
 12      print('Hello World')
 13      return message
 14
```

The preceding code will display a `Hello World` message whenever the Lambda function gets triggered. This we have completed the setup for this task.

13. To test the preceding setup, you can simply upload more than five files to your `receiver-bucket` bucket and check for Lambda function's execution.

SQS trigger

The **AWS Simple Queue Service (SQS)** is the AWS queue service. This service is similar to the queuing mechanisms that are used generally in software engineering. This enables us to add, store, and remove messages inside the queue.

We will learn how to trigger a Lambda function, depending on the number of messages in a SQS queue. This task will help you understand how serverless batch data architectures can be built and how to build one yourself.

We will do this by monitoring our SQS queue with a CloudWatch alarm and relaying the information to Lambda via an SNS topic, just like we did in the previous task.

So, in this section, we will do the following:

1. Create an SQS queue
2. Create an SNS topic
3. Create a CloudWatch alarm for our SQS queue to monitor the number of messages in the queue
4. Once the messages count reaches 5, the alarm will be set to **ALERT** and the corresponding notification will be sent to the SNS topic we have just created
5. This SNS topic will then trigger a Lambda function, which prints out a `Hello World` message for us

This will help you understand how to monitor queues and build efficient serverless data architectures that are batched, instead of in real time.

The process flow for this is as follows:

1. We will start by creating an AWS SQS queue. We need to go to the SQS dashboard of our AWS account. The dashboard looks like this:

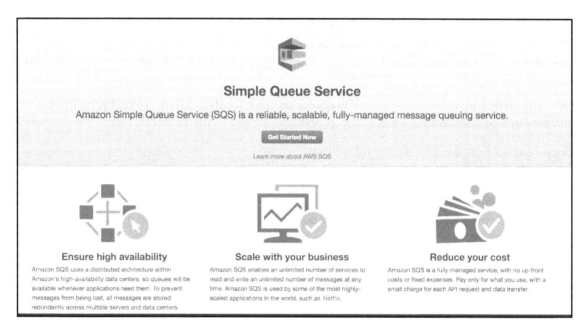

2. Click on the **Get Started Now** button to create an SQS queue. It will redirect you to the queue creation wizard, where you need to enter details such as the name, type of queue, and so on. The queue creation wizard looks like this:

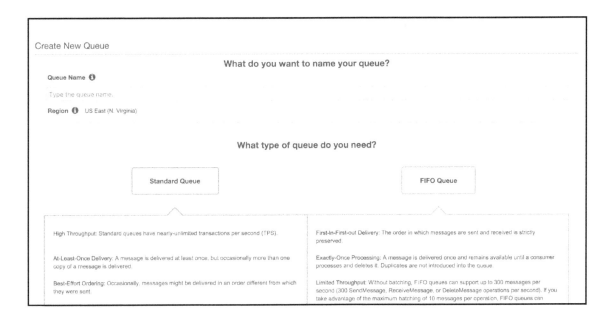

3. You can enter the name of the queue in **Queue Name**. In the **What type of queue do you need?** option, select the **Standard Queue** option. In the options at the bottom, select the blue **Quick-Create Queue** option:

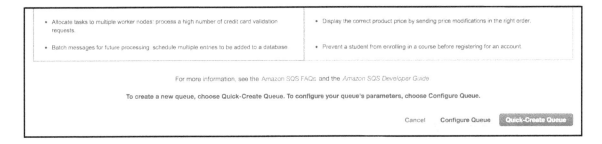

The **Configure Queue** option is for advanced settings. It is not necessary to tweak those settings for this task. This is what the advanced settings look like:

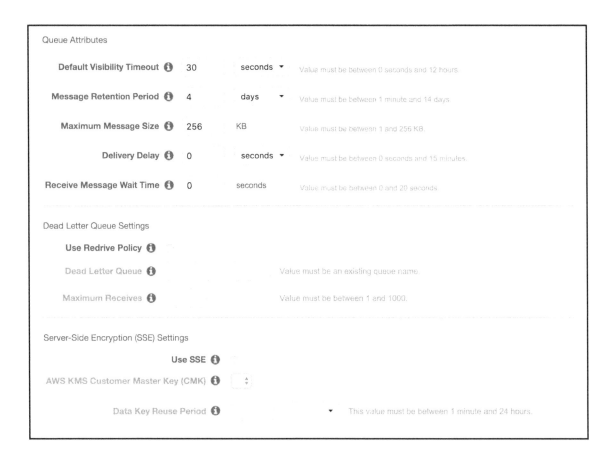

5. Once you have created the queue, you will be taken to the SQS page, where all the queues that you have created are listed similarly to the SNS list. This page looks like this:

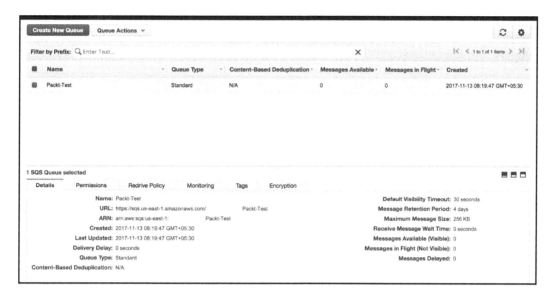

6. As we have already created an SNS topic in the previous task, we will use the same topic for this purpose. If you haven't created an SNS topic, you can refer to the previous task for instructions on how to create one. The list of SNS topics looks like this:

7. Now, we will go to the **CloudWatch** dashboard to create an alarm to monitor our SQS queue and send a notification to Lambda via the SNS topic that we have already created. We can now see the SQS queue metrics in the alarm creation wizard:

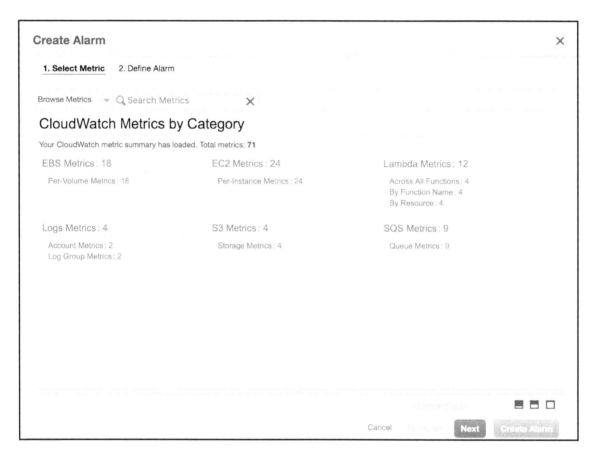

8. By clicking on the **Queue Metrics** option under **SQS Metrics**, we will be taken to the page where all queue metrics are listed, and we need to select one of them for our alarm:

9. Here, we are interested in the **ApproximateNumberOfMessagesVisible** metric,
    which gives the number of messages in the queue. It says Approximate, as SQS is
    a distributed queue and the number of messages can only be determined
    stochastically.

10. In the next page, after selecting the
    ApproximateNumberOfMessagesVisible metric from the list, the necessary
    settings can be configured as we did for the **S3 Metrics** in the previous task. The
    page should look like this:

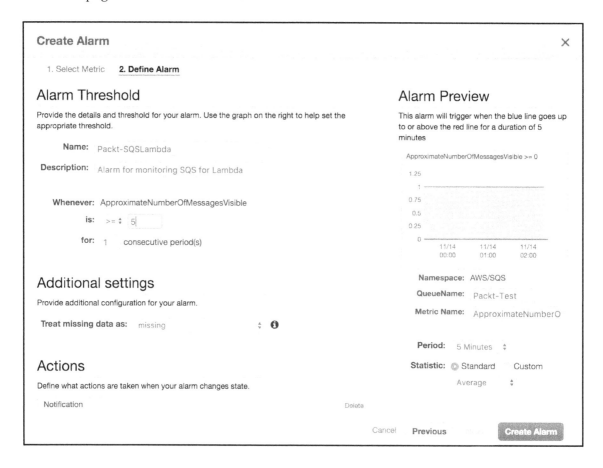

11. In the **Actions** section, configure the SNS topic to which we want to send our notification. This step is also similar to how we configured the SNS topic in the previous task:

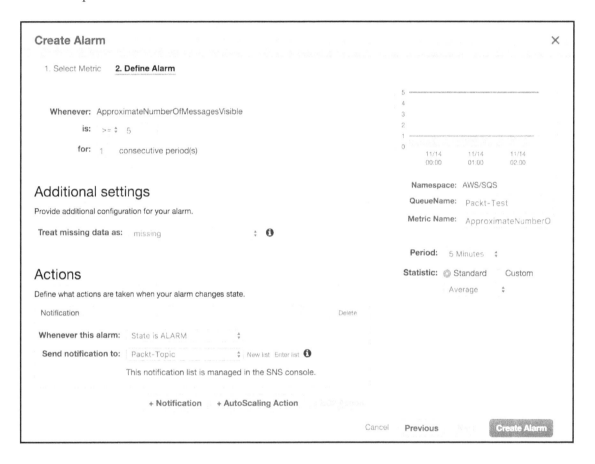

12. Once you are satisfied with the metadata and the settings you have configured for the alarm, you can click the blue **Create Alarm** button on the bottom-right side of the screen. That will successfully create an alarm that monitors your SQS queue and sends a notification to the SNS topic that you have configured:

13. We can use the Lambda function that we created in the previous task. Make sure the trigger is the SNS topic that we are using to configure the notification system of the alarm:

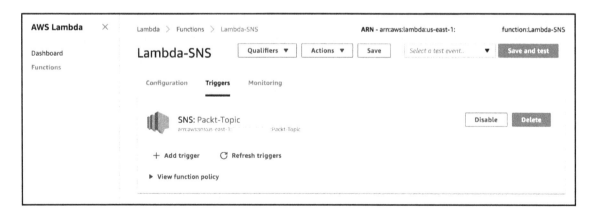

14. The Lambda function code for this task is as follows:

```
from __future__ import print_function
import json
print('Loading function')
def lambda_handler(event, context):
    #print("Received event: " + json.dumps(event, indent=2))
    message = event['Records'][0]['Sns']['Message']
    print("From SNS: " + message)
    print('Hello World')
    return message
```

CloudWatch trigger

CloudWatch is the logging and monitoring service for AWS, where logs from most services get stored and monitored. In this section, we will learn how CloudWatch trigger works, how CloudWatch querying works in practice, configuring this in the Lambda function, and also how to make use of this knowledge to build a Lambda function.

So, in this section, we will do the following:

1. Create a CloudWatch log
2. Briefly understand how a CloudWatch log works
3. Create a Lambda function that gets triggered by the CloudWatch trigger

This will help you understand and build resilient and stable serverless architectures.

The process flow for this is as follows:

1. To create a CloudWatch Logs group, click on the **Logs** option to the left of the **CloudWatch** console:

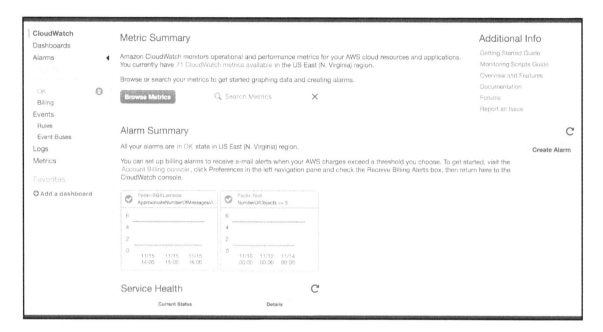

2. Once you are on the AWS CloudWatch **Logs** page, you will see a list of log groups that are already present. The CloudWatch **Logs** page looks something like this:

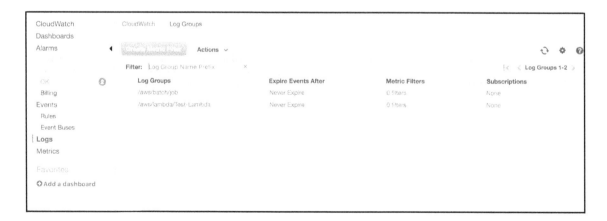

3. Let's go ahead and create a new CloudWatch log. You can see the option to create a new log group from the **Actions** drop-down menu at the top:

4. In the next step, you will be asked to name the log group that you are creating. Go ahead and enter the relevant information and click **Create log group**:

5. So, now we have a new log group listed in the list of log groups in our **CloudWatch** console:

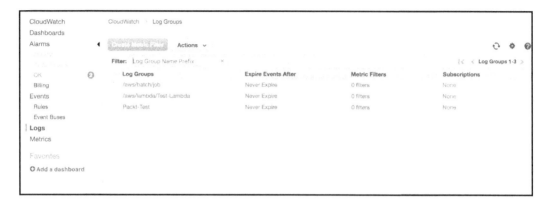

6. Once the log group has been created, we can now start working on our Lambda function. So, let's move on to the Lambda console and start creating a new function.

7. From the blueprints, choose the **cloudwatch-logs-process-data** blueprint. The description reads: **A real-time consumer of log events ingested by an Amazon CloudWatch Logs log group**:

8. After selecting the corresponding blueprint option, you will be redirected to the Lambda creation wizard, as usual:

9. Just as we did in the previous task, we will also enter relevant information about the log name and other details in the **cloudwatch-logs** pane of the Lambda creation panel:

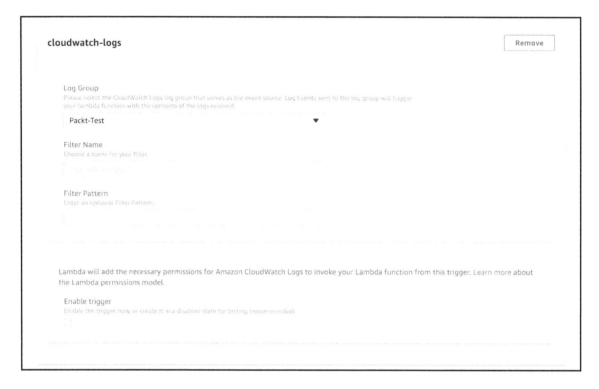

10. After clicking **Create function**, we will be directed to a **Triggers** page with the success message.

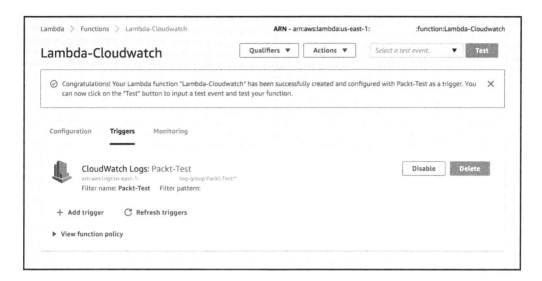

11. So, now we write the Lambda function code to identify the log group and print `Hello World` message:

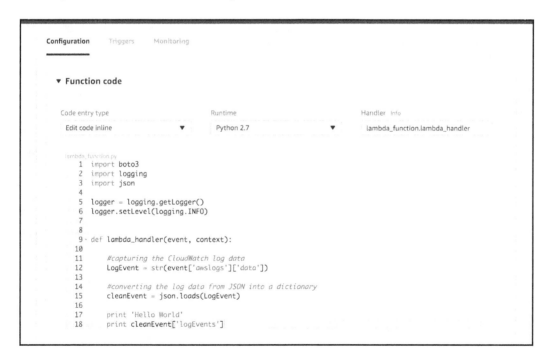

12. We have now successfully completed another task where we understood how to trigger a Lambda function via AWS CloudWatch Logs. The Lambda function code for this task is as follows:

```
import boto3
import logging
import json
logger = logging.getLogger()
logger.setLevel(logging.INFO)
def lambda_handler(event, context):
#capturing the CloudWatch log data
LogEvent = str(event['awslogs']['data'])
#converting the log data from JSON into a dictionary
cleanEvent = json.loads(LogEvent)
print 'Hello World'
print cleanEvent['logEvents']
```

Summary

In this chapter, we have learned a great deal about how various Lambda triggers work, and how to configure them, set up the triggers, and write Lambda function code to handle the data from them.

In the first task, we learned how S3 events work and how to understand and receive events from the S3 service to AWS Lambda. We have understood how to monitor S3 buckets for file details via their metrics in CloudWatch and then send that notification via AWS SNS to a Lambda functions.

We have also learned how to create SNS topics and how to use them as an intermediate route between several metrics of AWS services from CloudWatch to AWS Lambda.

We have learned briefly about how AWS CloudWatch works. We understood what the metrics of various AWS services, such as S3, SQS, and CloudWatch, look like. We also learned how to set thresholds for CloudWatch Alarms, and how to connect those alarms to notification services, such as AWS SNS.

We learned how AWS CloudWatch Logs work and how to connect and use the CloudWatch trigger in Lambda so it's triggered whenever a new log event is added/received. Overall, we have successfully created new AWS services, such as SQS, CloudWatch Logs, SNS, and S3 buckets in this chapter, and successfully built and deployed three serverless tasks/pipelines.

In the next chapter, we will learn how to build serverless APIs, on which we will perform some tasks just like we did in this chapter, and get a hands-on understanding of how APIs work and, most importantly, how serverless APIs work.

.

Deploying Serverless APIs 4

So far, we have come a long way in our journey of learning about serverless applications and building serverless engineering. We have learned what the serverless paradigm actually is, how the AWS Lambda function works, understanding the internals of AWS Lambda, along with a detailed understanding of how several triggers work. We have also done several mini projects around experimenting with triggers and deploying them as end-to-end serverless pipelines.

In this chapter, you will be learning how to build efficient and scalable serverless APIs, using the AWS Lambda and AWS API Gateway services. We will start with understanding how the API Gateway works, instead of diving directly to building the serverless API. After that, we will understand how API Gateway and AWS Lambda integrate with each other. And finally, we will be creating and deploying a fully functional serverless API, as part of your learning from this chapter.

This chapter covers the following topics:

- API methods and resources
- Setting up integration
- Deploying the Lambda function for API execution
- Handling authentication and user controls

API methods and resources

In this section, we will be learning about the API service of AWS, which is the API Gateway, and understanding the components and settings available in the console for the user who is creating APIs. We will go through all of the components and understand the API Gateway better. The steps to create the serverless APIs are as follows:

1. We will start by opening the API Gateway console, which looks like this:

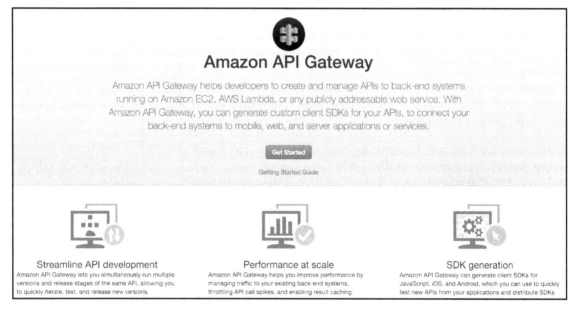

2. In the API Gateway console, click on the **Get Started** button to start creating an API. It will take you to an API creation wizard with a popup saying **Create Example API**:

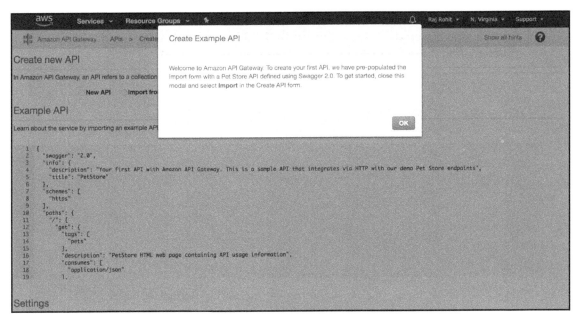

3. Once you click on the **OK** button, you will be redirected to a page where the **Example API** is shown, from which you can get an idea of what an API response looks like:

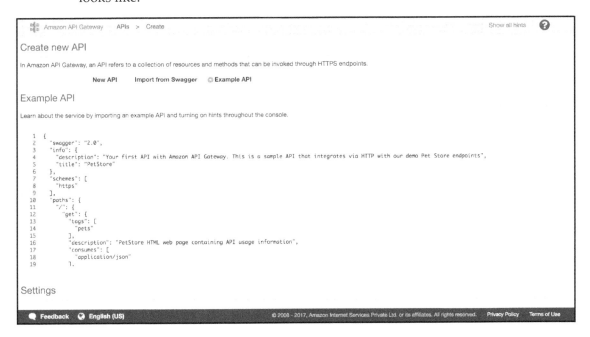

The API we are building in this example is for a pet store and for maintaining the pets inside the store. By going through the API, you will see what the bits and pieces of an API looks like. The API looks like this:

```
        Amazon API Gateway    APIs  >  Create                                    Show all hints    ?

Example API

Learn about the service by importing an example API and turning on hints throughout the console.

 1  {
 2    "swagger": "2.0",
 3    "info": {
 4      "description": "Your first API with Amazon API Gateway. This is a sample API that integrates via HTTP with our demo Pet Store endpoints",
 5      "title": "PetStore"
 6    },
 7    "schemes": [
 8      "https"
 9    ],
10    "paths": {
11      "/": {
12        "get": {
13          "tags": [
14            "pets"
15          ],
16          "description": "PetStore HTML web page containing API usage information",
17          "consumes": [
18            "application/json"
19          ],
```

4. Once you click on the **Import** button at the end, you will be redirected to the **PetStore (b7exp0d681)** API page that we have just created. The API page with all the components looks like this:

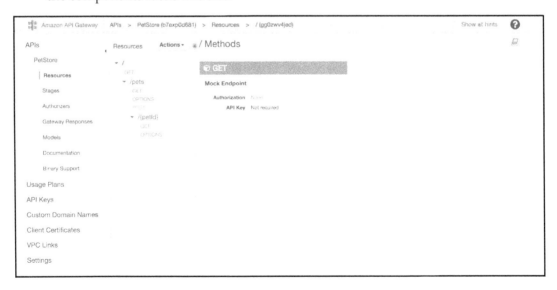

5. The resources in this API are the **GET** and **POST** resources, where you can add pets and view the pets, which are available as a list. The list of resources from the API we have created is as follows:

6. By clicking on the first **GET** resource, we can see a detailed execution flow from the client to the endpoint and back to the client. The execution flow of the resource looks like this:

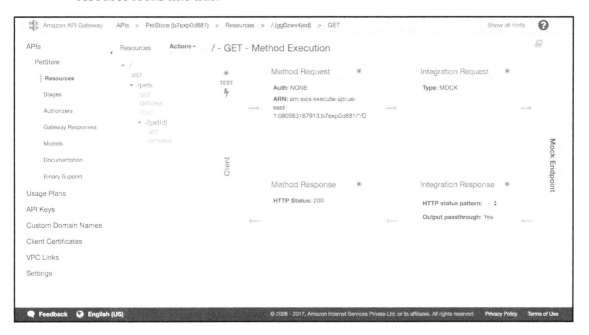

7. Now, if we click on the **POST** resource, we will find a similar model execution flow for the **POST** resource. It looks very similar to that of the **GET** resource, however, here the API endpoint is mentioned as a URL, as we are trying to retrieve the result from it. The execution model looks as follows:

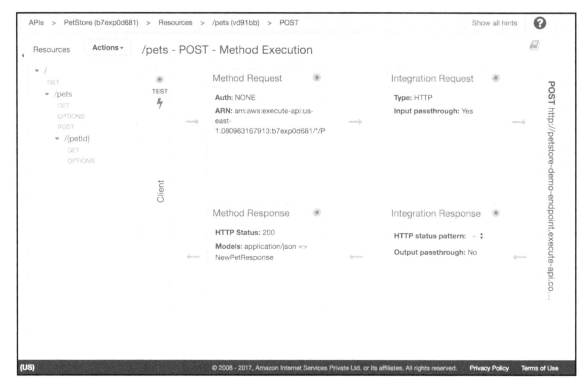

In the API Gateway, there is something called **Stages**, which can be used as versioning models for an API. Some common names for **Stages** in practice are **test**, **development**, and **production**. The **Stages** menu looks like this:

7. When you click on the **Create** option, it will open a creation wizard for the stage. This looks as follows:

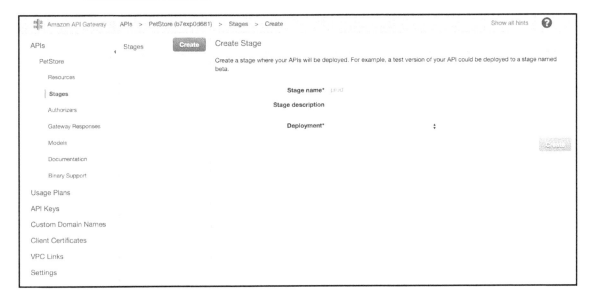

8. You can select any name for the **Stage name** value, and add the **Stage description** value according to the name you have assigned and the purpose you have in mind for this stage. Before that, you need to deploy the API that you have created. This can be selected in the **Actions** drop-down menu as the **Deploy API** button, as follows:

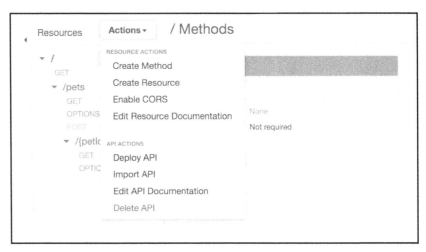

9. In the next menu, you can choose the **Stage name** and other details, before finally clicking on the **Deploy** button, which will deploy your API with that particular stage. This can be seen as follows:

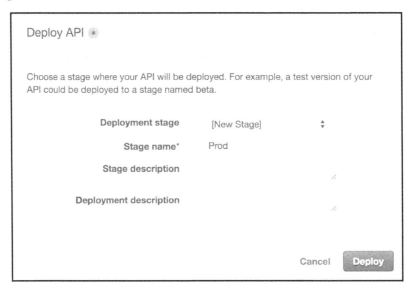

The deployed stage would look as follows:

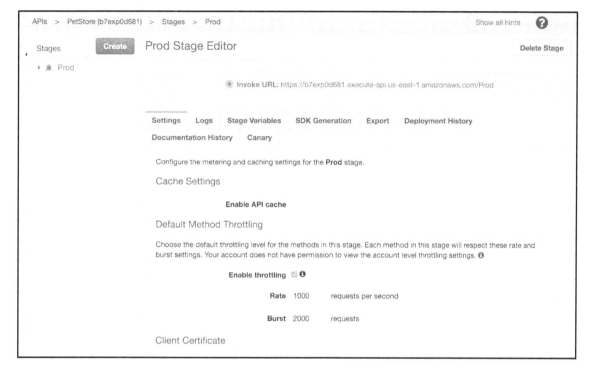

Setting up integration

As we now understand how the AWS API Gateway service works at a basic level, we will move on to use that knowledge for building an end-to-end project which involves deploying a completely serverless API.

In this section, we will be building and deploying a completely serverless API function from scratch, along with learning the internals and other implementation details of the AWS Lambda—AWS API Gateway integrations. We will be building the serverless API step-by-step. So, follow along with the steps in this order. The procedure is as follows:

1. Firstly, we will start by creating a new API. This can be done via the Lambda console which looks like this:

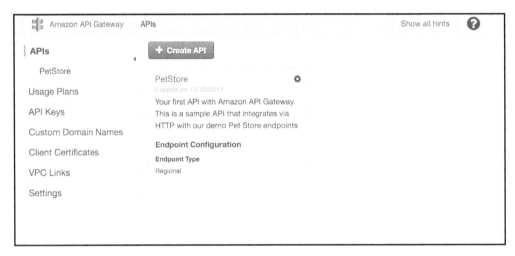

2. Once you have clicked on the **+Create API** button, you will be redirected to the API creation wizard, where you will be asked to enter the name and description of the API you are intending to build. For now, I have entered the name as `TestLambdaAPI`. However, you are free to add whatever name and description you would like to enter. The API creation console looks like this:

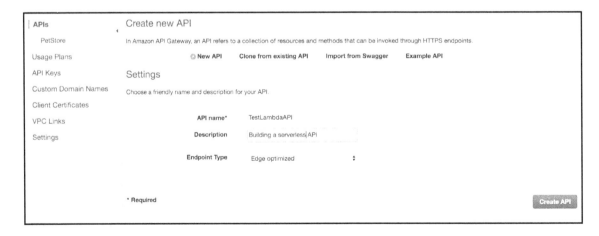

3. Once you click on the **Create API** button, you will be redirected to the page of the API you have created. The API page would look similar to this:

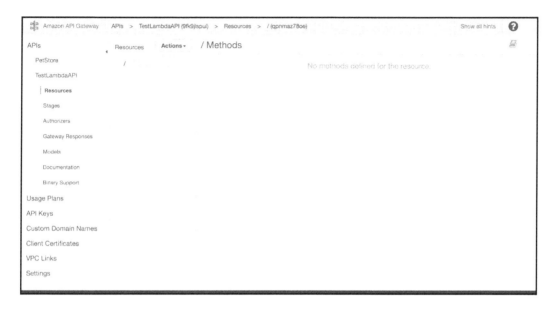

4. Now that we have successfully created an API, we will now go ahead and create resources in the API. You can do that by clicking on the **Create Resource** option in the **Actions** drop-down menu:

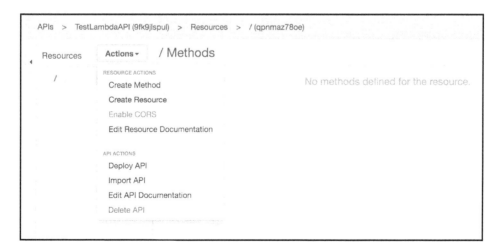

5. This would open up a resource creation wizard where you can add the name and resource path of the API resource which we are intending to build. After creating the resource, click on the **Create Resource** button for your settings for the API resource to be created accordingly. For the sake of this tutorial, I have named it `LambdaAPI`. However, you can give it any name you want. The API creation wizard looks like this:

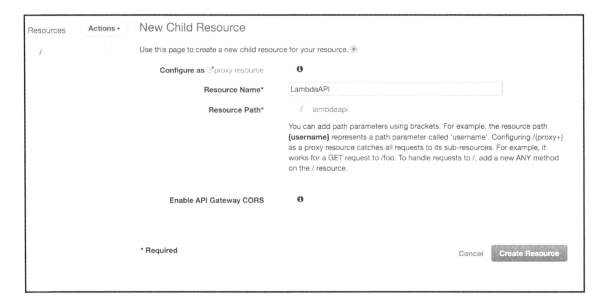

The resource that you have just created is now live in the API console; you can see it under the **Resources** section:

6. You can create versions of a resource or even just a resource under a resource. Let's go ahead and create one. For this, you need to click on the resource that you have already created. Then, click on the **Create Resource** option in the drop-down menu in the **Actions** menu:

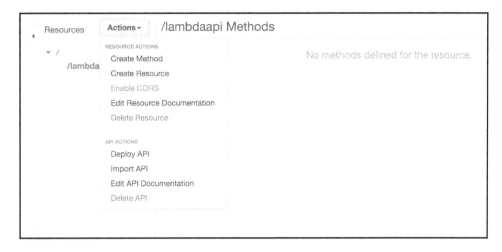

7. This would open up a similar resource creation wizard under the resource which we have already created. You can name that resource as `version1` or just as `v1` which is a regular software practice. I have named it `v1`. However, you can name it whatever you want to:

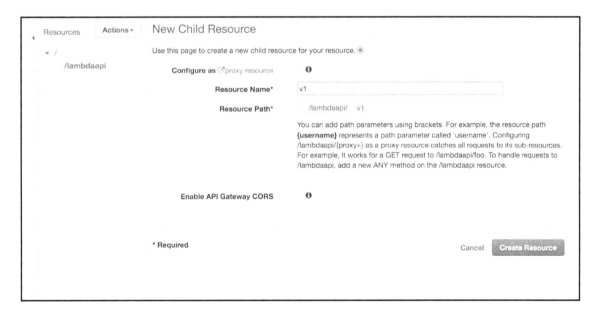

Now, we have a resource named `v1` under the already existing resource, `/lambdaapi`. We can see this under our **Resources** section. So, now the resources hierarchy of our API looks like this:

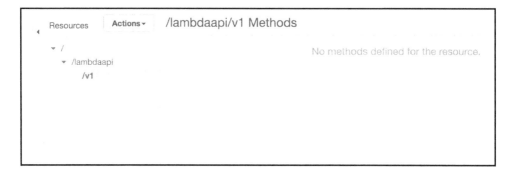

8. We will be creating a serverless API for getting and querying the list of pets in a pet store. So, the following steps will be aligned accordingly. The API should return the name of the pets. So, we will have a new resource for pets for that purpose. We will be creating a resource for this under the `/v1` resource:

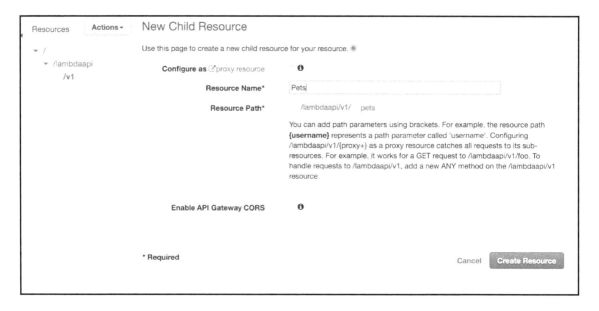

9. The resulting hierarchical structure for our API looks like this, after adding the /pets resource under the /v1 resource:

10. Now, we will add a custom resource which enables us to query the API. By custom, we mean that any string can be added to the resource when sending a request to this API, and the API would send back a request after checking and querying for that string via a Lambda code. The custom resources can be differentiated from the normal ones, as they can be created with curly braces. The following screenshot will help you understand how to create them:

11. After clicking on the **Create Resource** button, the new custom child resource for /pets will be created. The hierarchy of the resources is now as follows:

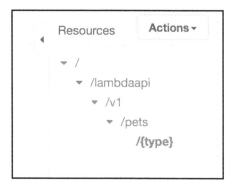

12. The overall structure of the API looks like this, as specified in the top-right part of the following screenshot:

13. Now, we will add methods to this custom resource. As we will only be querying the list of pets, we will only add the **GET** method. This can be done by clicking on the {type} resource and clicking on **Create Method** in the drop-down **Actions** menu in the top panel:

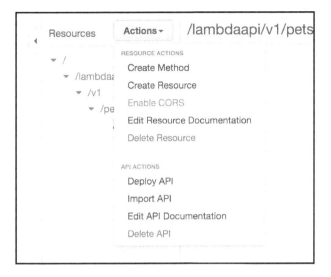

14. This would create a small drop-down style menu under the **{type}** resource where you can select a method from the available methods:

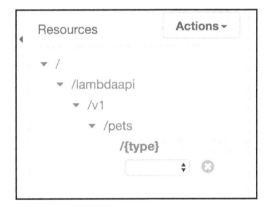

15. We need to select the **GET** option from the available options. This would look as follows:

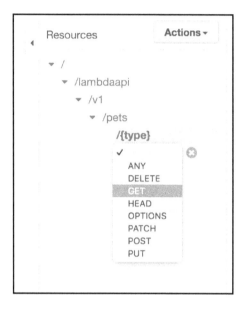

16. After selecting the **GET** option and clicking on the small tick button beside it, we will have created the **GET** method under our **{type}** resource. The hierarchy now looks like this:

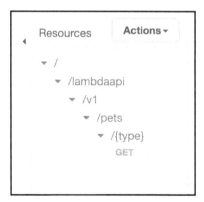

Deploying the Lambda function for API execution

In this section, we will have a look at the steps to deploy the Lambda function:

1. The details of the **GET** method can also be seen on the right-hand side of the API console, when you click on that method. The details look as follows:

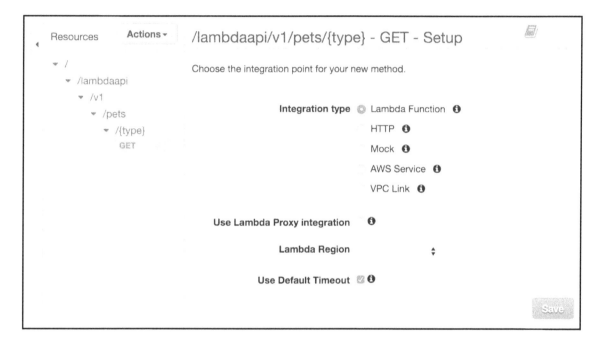

2. In the **GET** method console, click on the **Lambda Function** option. Select any one region depending on your preference. I have chosen **us-east-1** as the region as shown in the following screenshot:

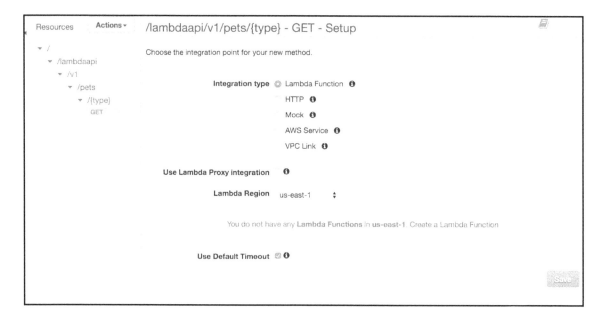

3. As expected, it says we do not have a Lambda function in that region. So, we need to go ahead and create one. Click on the **Create a Lambda Function** link. This will take you to the Lambda creation console which we are already comfortable with:

4. From here, choose the **keyword : hello-world-python** blueprint from the list of blueprints:

5. In the next console, choose the basic information for the Lambda function as we have done in the previous chapters:

6. After adding the relevant details, click on the orange **Create function** button. That will take you to the page of the Lambda function you have just created. The code can be edited from there onwards:

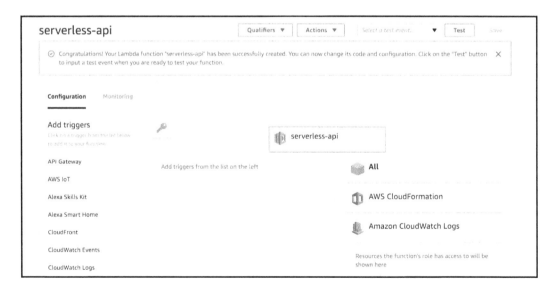

7. In the function's code, use this code instead of the one which is provided along with the blueprint:

```python
def lambda_handler(event, context):
    mobs = {
        "Sea": ["GoldFish", "Turtle", "Tortoise", "Dolphin", "Seal"],
        "Land": ["Labrador", "Cat", "Dalmatian", "German Shepherd",
                    "Beagle", "Golden Retriever"],
        "Exotic": ["Iguana", "Rock Python"]
    }

    return {"type": mobs[event['type']]}
```

8. We are now done with tweaking the function code. Now, you can go ahead and save the function:

9. Now, head back to the API Gateway console to the **GET** method page. Here, under the Lambda functions in the **us-east-1** region, I start getting the Lambda function which I have just created (**serverless-api**) as an option:

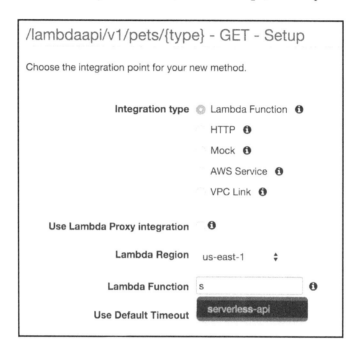

10. On clicking **Save**, you will see a popup asking you to confirm that you are giving API Gateway permission to invoke your Lambda function, you can acknowledge it by clicking on **OK**:

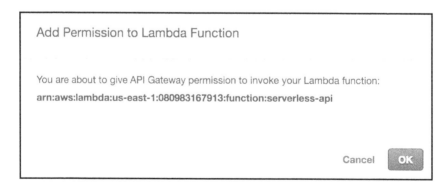

11. After clicking on **OK**, you will be redirected to the data flow page of the **GET** method, that looks like this:

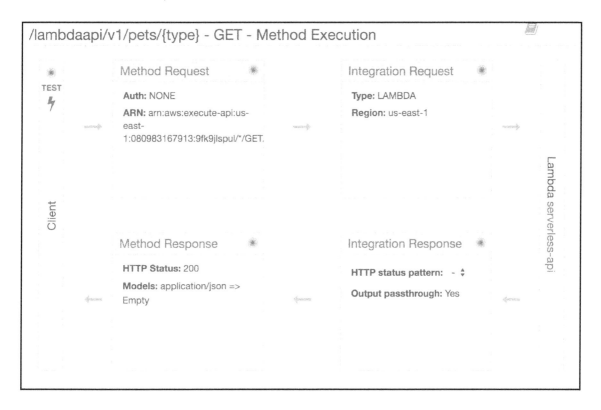

Handling authentication and user controls

After deploying, next we will discuss how to handle the authentication and user controls. The steps are as follows:

1. Now that we have successfully created the skeleton of our serverless API, we will now work on the nitty-gritty details which are needed to make it a fully functional API. We will start with applying the mapping templates. This can be done in the **Integration Request** menu. Clicking on the **Integration Request** link will take you to a console which looks like this:

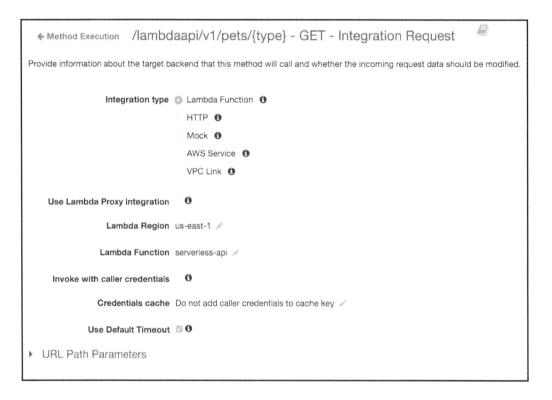

2. If you scroll down a bit in the same console, you will notice the **Body Mapping Templates** section at the end:

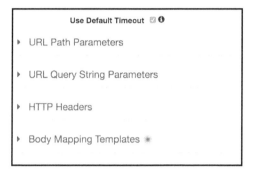

3. Clicking on the **Body Mapping Templates** will unfurl the options available in that particular section:

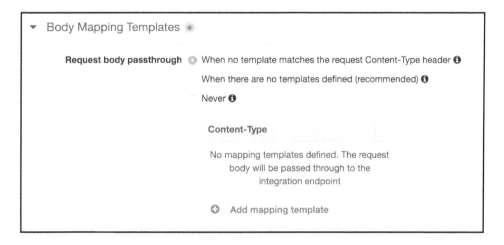

4. Select the second option which says **When there are no templates defined (recommended)**. And then, click on the **Add mapping template** option and add `application/json`, and click on the small grey tick symbol beside it:

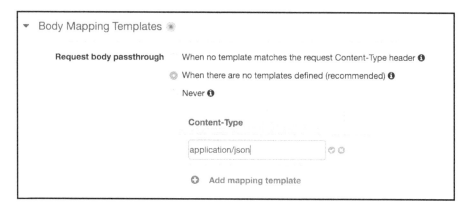

5. After clicking the small grey tick symbol beside it, the **Body Mapping Templates** section space will look like this:

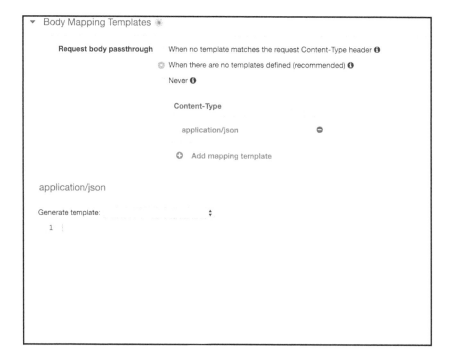

6. Now, in the template textbox, add the following code and click the **Save** button underneath the text box:

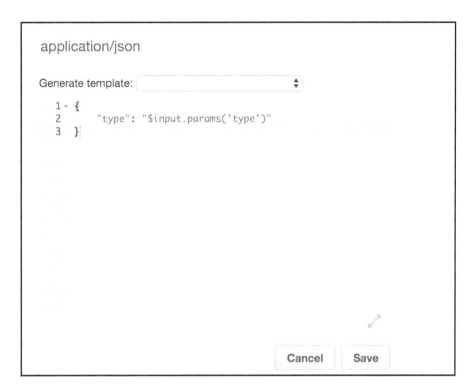

7. So, after all these steps, the resulting **Body Mapping Templates** section will look like this:

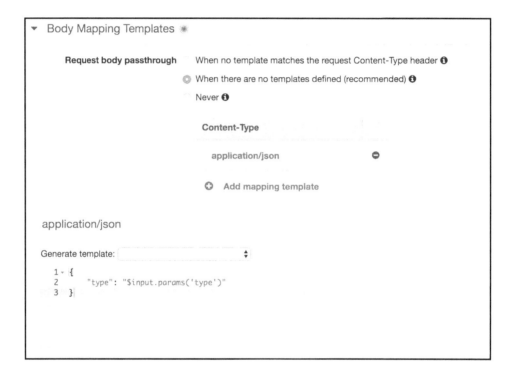

8. Now, going back to the **Method Execution** page, we can see the **TEST** option on the left with a lightning bolt symbol beneath it:

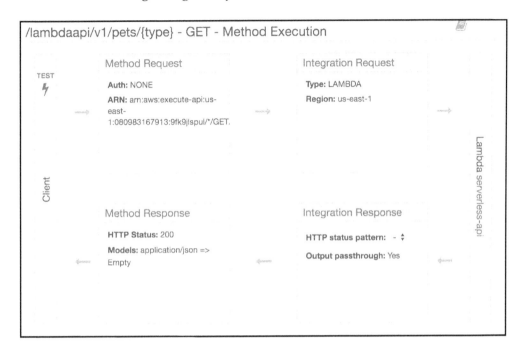

9. Clicking on the **TEST** button on the left-side in the **Client** section and above the thunderbolt option will take you to a page where you can test the API that you've just created:

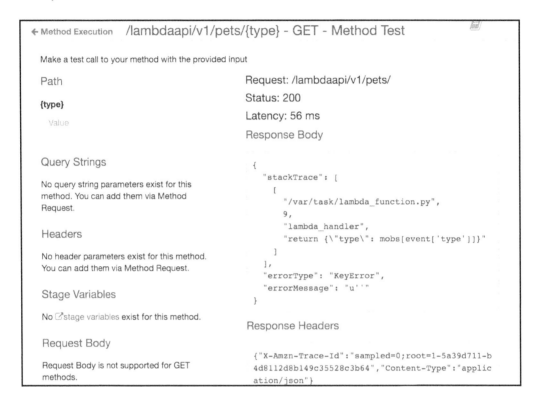

10. Now, let's type `Exotic` in the textbox below **{type}** and click on the **Test** button at the bottom. If everything goes right, we should see the list of all the exotic pets we have entered in the function code of our Lambda function:

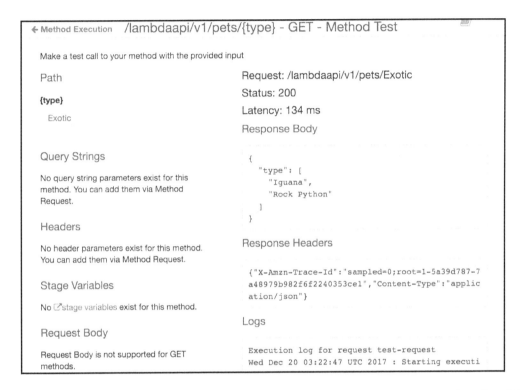

11. And rightly so, we did get the list of all of the exotic pets in the catalog. So, this brings this chapter to an end, where you have learned how to build a fully fledged serverless API from scratch, including how to deploy it.

12. In addition, if you want to add additional security settings, such as **Authorizations** and **API Key Required**, you can do it in the **Method Request** menu:

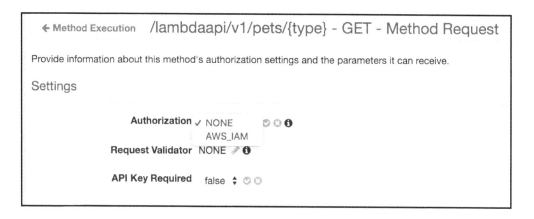

Summary

In this chapter, we have learned how to build a completely serverless API from scratch. We have also learned how to add more resources and methods for the API, as well as how to deploy it successfully to multiple stages of development and how to add additional security settings such as authorization and API keys for authentication purposes.

We then learned how to associate a Lambda function with our API Gateway's API service for handling the computational tasks of our API.

In the next chapter, we will be learning about logging and monitoring serverless applications. In that chapter, we will learn about the logging and monitoring services of AWS such as CloudWatch Metrics, CloudWatch Logs, and CloudWatch Dashboards in detail, and try to set them up for our serverless applications. We will also learn how to create a logging and monitoring pipeline from AWS Lambda to these monitoring tools using some AWS services.

5
Logging and Monitoring

We have learned about the concepts of serverless architectures and understood the basics and the internals of AWS's serverless service, AWS Lambda. We have also created some example serverless projects to understand the concepts better. During the course of our learning, we have also learned the basics of several other AWS services, such as alarms, SNS, SQS, S3 buckets, and CloudWatch.

In this chapter, we will learn about how to do the logging and monitoring for the serverless systems that we are building. Logging and monitoring software code and systems are very important, as they helps us with the telemetry and disaster recovery. Logging is a process where we store the logs emitted by our code or by our architecture as a whole. Monitoring is a process where we closely monitor the activities, status, and health of the components and processes in our code or architecture.

So, you will be learning how to set up and understand the monitoring suite of AWS Lambda, which is closely integrated with the monitoring service of AWS, the CloudWatch Dashboards. We will also learn about the logging service of AWS, the CloudWatch Logs service. Finally, we will also learn about and understand the distributed tracing and monitoring service of AWS, the CloudTrail service.

This chapter covers the following topics:

- Understanding CloudWatch
- Understanding CloudTrail
- Lambda's metrics in CloudWatch
- Lambda's logs in CloudWatch
- Logging statements in Lambda

Understanding CloudWatch

As mentioned earlier, CloudWatch is the logging and monitoring service of AWS. We have already looked at and learned about the CloudWatch Alarms, which are a sub-feature of CloudWatch. We will now learn about the graphing suite of the service. Almost every service in the AWS environment has a way to send it's logs and metrics to CloudWatch for logging and monitoring purposes. Each service might have several metrics which can be monitored, depending on the function.

Similarly, AWS Lambda also has some metrics, such as the invocation count, the invocation's running time, and so on, which it sends to CloudWatch. It is also helpful to note that the developers can also send custom metrics to CloudWatch. So in the following steps, we shall be learning about the different parts and functions of AWS CloudWatch corresponding to AWS Lambda:

1. Firstly, let us see what the CloudWatch console looks like and also get a feel for it by navigating around the console. Browse to `console.aws.amazon.com/cloudwatch/`:

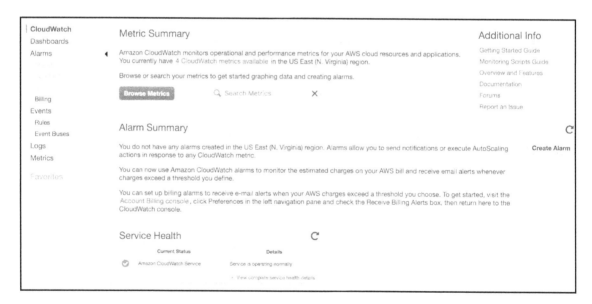

2. As we can see, there is a lot of information in the CloudWatch console. So, we shall now try to understand each component one after the other. In the left side, we can see a list of options, which includes **Dashboards**, **Alarms**, **Billing**, and so on. We shall try to understand all of them and their functionality as part of understanding the CloudWatch console.

3. A dashboard here is a panel of CloudWatch Metrics that the user can configure. For example, a user might want to have a particular set of server (EC2) metrics at a single place to be able to monitor them better. This is where AWS CloudWatch Dashboards come into play. When you click on the **Dashboards** option on the left, you can see the **Dashboards** console, which looks like this:

4. Let us go ahead and create a new dashboard by clicking the blue **Create dashboard** button on the top left-hand side of the console. The following box appears:

5. This will take you to the next step, where you will be asked to select a widget type for the dashboard. There are four types of widgets which are currently available. The widget selection screen looks like this:

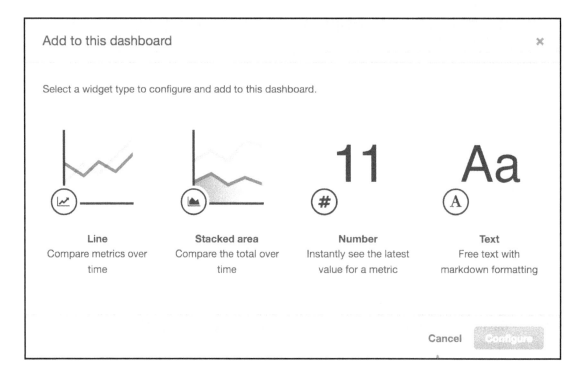

6. For the sake of this tutorial, I am choosing the **Line** style widget. You can choose whatever widget would fit your graphing style and the monitoring you need to do. Once you select a widget style and click the blue **Configure** button, you will be redirected to a wizard where you will be asked to add a metric as shown in the following screenshot:

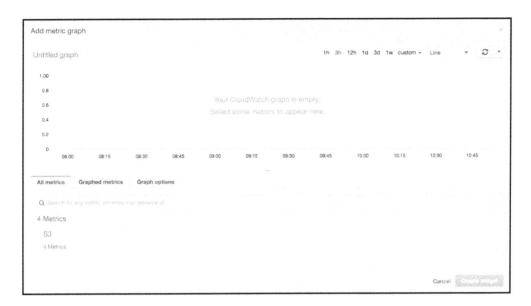

7. Select one of the available metrics at the bottom and it will be added to the widget. Once you are done with selecting the metrics, click on the blue **Create widget** button in the lower-right part of the page as shown in the following screenshot:

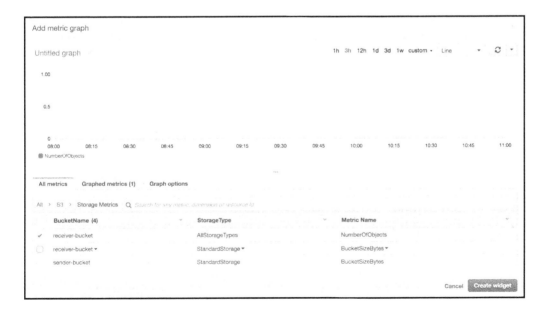

8. Now, you can see the dashboard that you have just created in the Dashboards section:

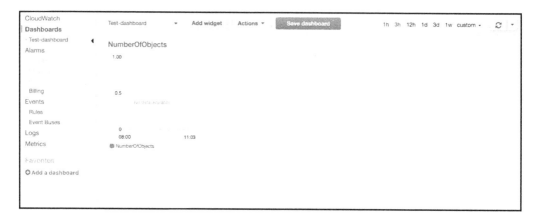

9. We have successfully learned and created an AWS CloudWatch Dashboard. We will now move on to learning about CloudWatch Events. We have already learned about CloudWatch Alarms in the previous chapters, looking at both their functionality and how to create and work with them.

10. Click on the **Events** link in the **CloudWatch** menu on the left. You will be redirected to the page of CloudWatch Events, as shown in the following screenshot:

11. Once you click on the blue **Create rule** button, you will be redirected to the **Events** creation wizard, which looks like this:

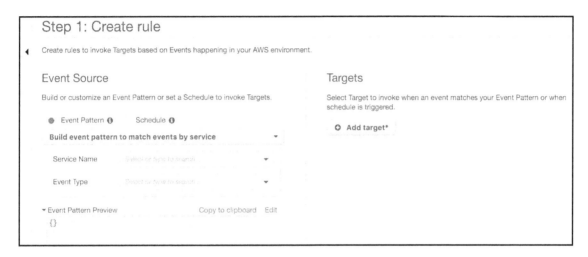

12. There can be two types of events, namely **Event Pattern** and **Schedule**, each of which have different purposes. Here we will only learn about the **Schedule** type, as it comes in handy for scheduling Lambda functions:

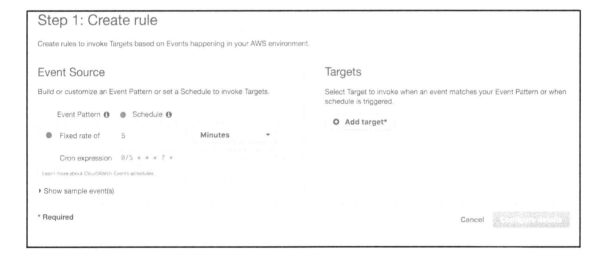

13. The rate can be either set in terms of **Minutes**, **Hours**, or **Days**, or can be set as a cron expression, whichever way you are comfortable with. Now, the target needs to be selected. The target can be any valid Lambda function, as shown in the following drop-down menu:

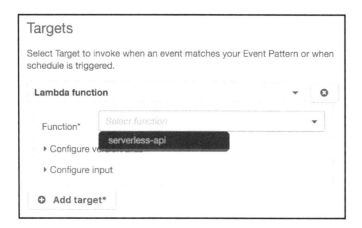

14. Once you have selected the function, you can click on the blue **Configure details** at the bottom. It will take you to the **Configure rule details** page as shown in the following screenshot:

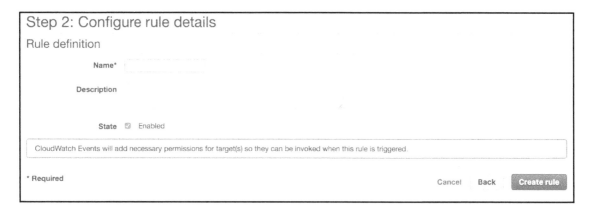

15. Once you enter the name and the description of the rule that you want to create, you can click on the blue **Create rule** button at the bottom. This will successfully create an event, and the same will be reflected in your CloudWatch console:

We have successfully added a cron event for a Lambda function which means that Lambda will be invoked at regular intervals, as specified by the user in the settings of the event.

16. Now, we shall try to understand the **Logs** feature of AWS CloudWatch. This is where the Lambda functions store their logs. You can click on the **Logs** link in the menu on the left-hand side to access the console of CloudWatch Logs:

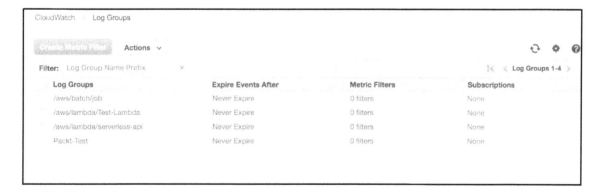

17. We can see the complete list of logs for all of the Lambda functions we have ever created throughout the course of the book. When you click on a log group, you can find more details about it, and also options for customization. Each log stream is an invocation of the Lambda function that the log is associated with:

18. You can also make use of the additional functionality provided by CloudWatch for handling the logs data, which can be seen in the drop-down **Actions** menu in **Log Groups**:

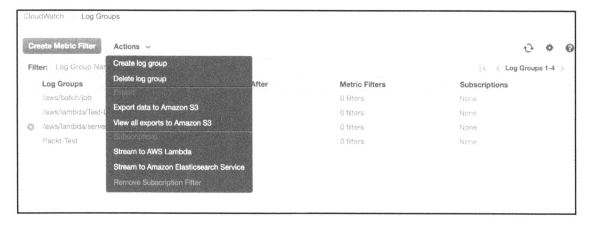

19. Finally, we will wrap up by exploring and learning about the CloudWatch Metrics. The metrics console can be accessed by clicking on the **Metrics** option on the left-hand side of the CloudWatch console:

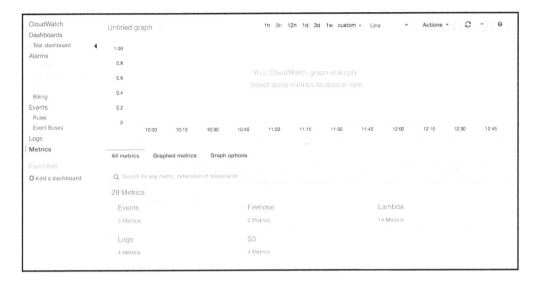

20. You can select any option in the menu at the bottom for graphing the metrics. For the purpose of this tutorial, I have added a Lambda metric, which is the number of errors in the function, `serverless-api`:

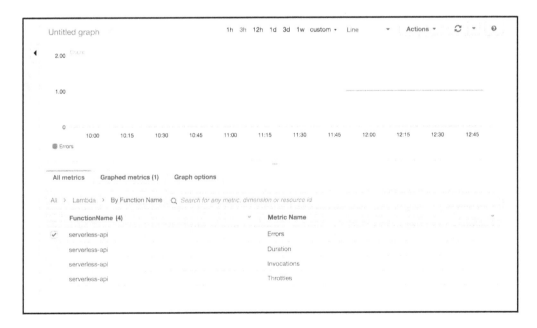

Understanding CloudTrail

CloudTrail is another monitoring service of AWS where you can look at all of the events and trails that have happened in your AWS account. This service is a bit more detailed than the CloudWatch service in how it records and stores the events and trails.

So, we shall explore and learn about this service in the following steps:

1. The AWS CloudTrail's dashboard can be accessed at
   `console.aws.amazon.com/cloudtrail/`:

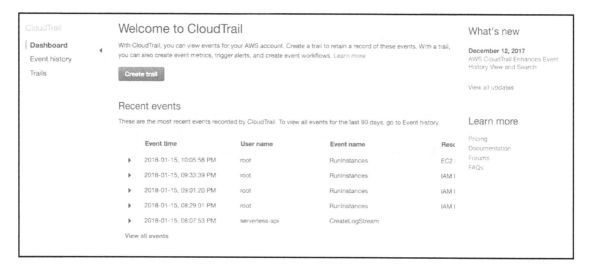

2. The list of events in your AWS account can be seen on the left-hand side of the **CloudTrail** menu when you click on the **Event history** button. The **Event history** page looks like this:

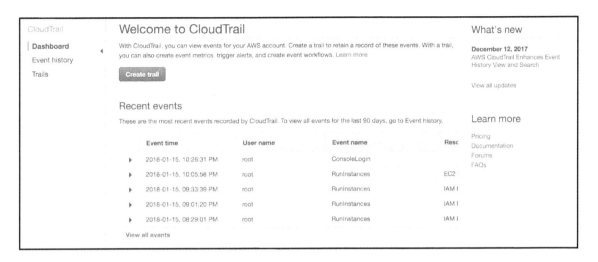

3. The third functionality of CloudTrail is the trails. The user can set up trails for their AWS services, such as Lambda. The trails that have been set up can be found on the **Trails** dashboard. This can be accessed by going to the **Trails** console by clicking on the **Trails** option in the menu on the left-hand side:

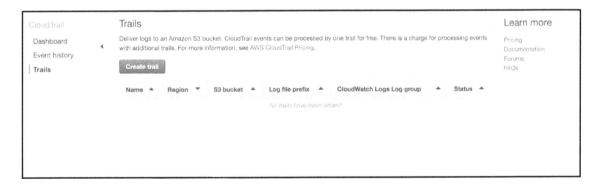

4. Now, let us understand how to create a trail in the **CloudTrail** dashboard. You can go to the main dashboard of CloudTrail and click on the blue **Create trail** button. This will take you to the trail creation wizard:

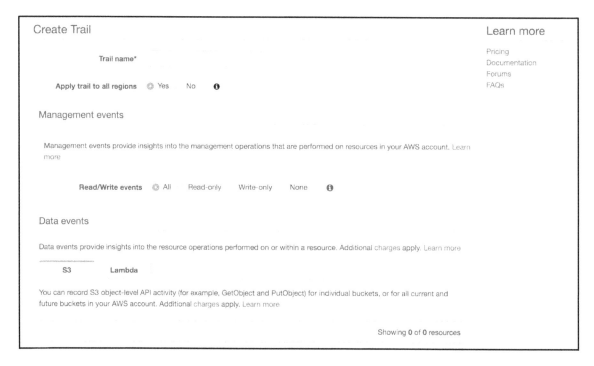

5. You can enter the details of your trail here. You can leave the default options as they are for the **Apply trail to all regions** and the **Management events** options:

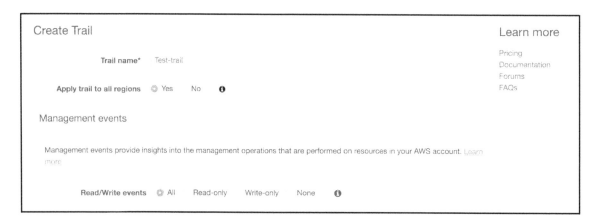

6. Now, moving on to the next setting, select the **Lambda** option and click on the **Log all current and future functions** in the options list. This will ensure that all of our Lambda functions are logged properly with CloudTrail:

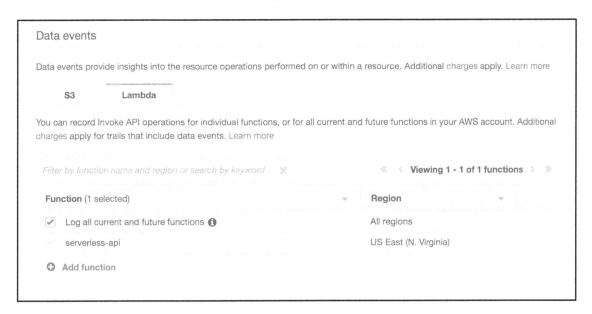

7. Now, in the final **Storage location** option, select an **S3 bucket** for storing the CloudTrail logs. This can be an already existing bucket or you can also ask CloudTrail to create a new bucket for this purpose. I am using an existing bucket:

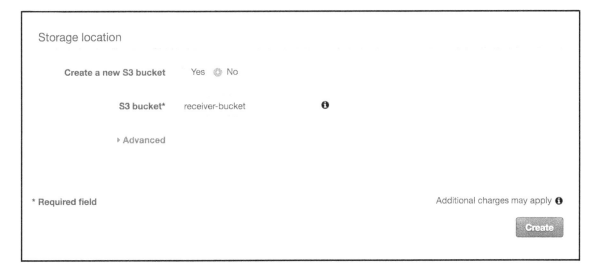

8. After all of the details and settings have been configured accordingly, you can click on the blue **Create trail** button to create the trail. Now, you see the trail you have just created in your **CloudTrail** dashboard as shown in the following screenshot:

9. Now, when you click on the trail that you have just created, you can see all of the details with which it has been configured as shown in the following screenshot:

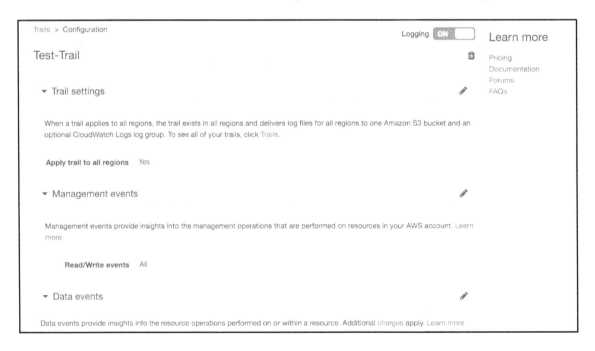

10. You can also notice a very interesting option that enables you to configure CloudWatch Logs along with SNS to notify you of any specific activities, for example when there is an error in a Lambda function:

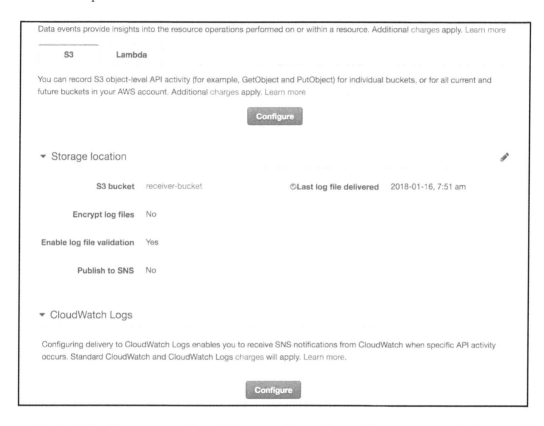

11. And finally, you can also add tags to the trail, just like you can with the rest of your AWS services:

12. Additionally, let us understand how to configure CloudWatch Logs for our trail. So, for this you need to click on the blue **Configure** button in the **CloudWatch Logs** section above the **Tags** section:

13. When you click **Continue**, it takes you to the creation wizard where you need to configure the permissions accordingly with your IAM role settings. For the purpose of this tutorial, I have selected the **Create a new IAM Role** option as shown in the following screenshot:

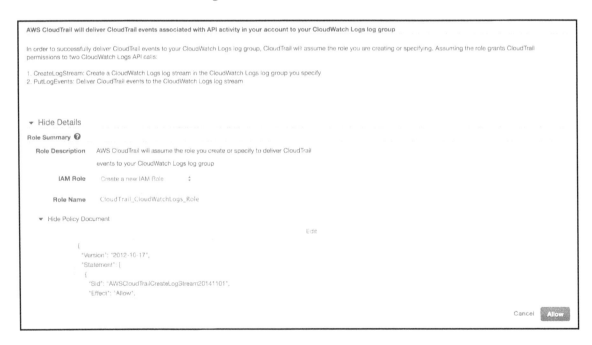

14. After you have finished configuring the IAM role settings, you can click on the blue **Allow** button at the bottom. After a couple of seconds of validation, the CloudWatch Logs get configured, which you can see in the same **CloudWatch Logs** section here:

Lambda's metrics in CloudWatch

As we have learned and understood how the CloudWatch and the CloudTrail services work with respect to logging and monitoring, we shall move on to try and implement them for our Lambda function(s). In this section, you will learn about the types of metrics that Lambda possesses, which are monitored by CloudWatch, and how to create a dashboard with all those metrics.

Similar to previous sections in this chapter and book, we shall try and understand the concepts in the form of the following steps:

1. When you navigate over to your AWS Lambda console, you will see the Lambda function which you have already created, in the list of available functions:

2. When you click on the function, you will see two available options on the top: **Configuration** and **Monitoring**. Navigate to the **Monitoring** section. You will see a dashboard of metrics, which contains the following:

- **Invocations**
- **Duration**
- **Errors**
- **Throttles**
- **Iterator age**
- **DLQ errors**

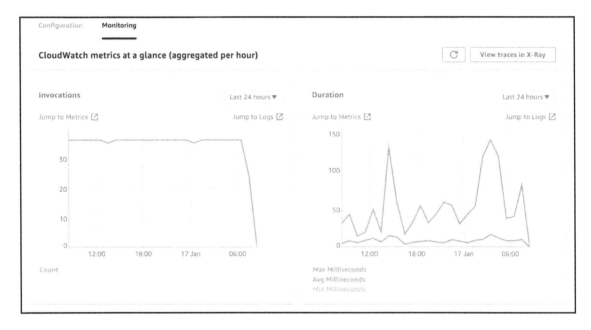

Invocations and duration

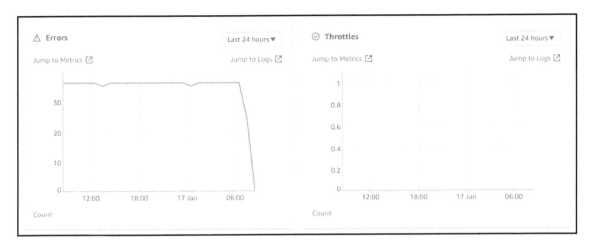

Errors and Throttles

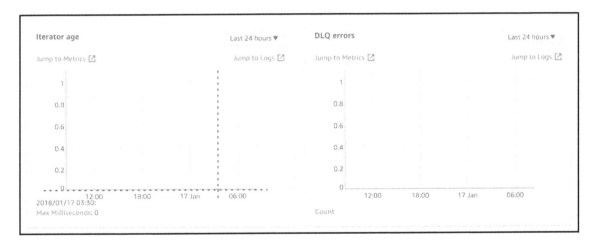

Iterator age and DLQ errors

3. Let us understand each of them in detail. The first metric is the **Invocations** metric, which has the time on the *x* axis and the number of invocations of the Lambda function on the *y* axis. This metric helps us understand when and how many times our Lambda function has been invocated:

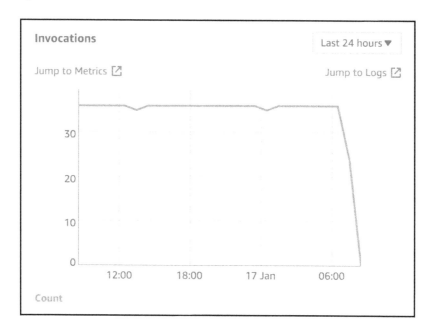

When you click **Jump to Logs**, it takes you to the CloudWatch Logs console of the Lambda invocations, which looks like this:

And when you click on the **Jump to Metrics** option, it will take you to the CloudWatch Metrics dashboard of that particular metric, which gives you a much more customized and granular graph of the same metric, which looks like this:

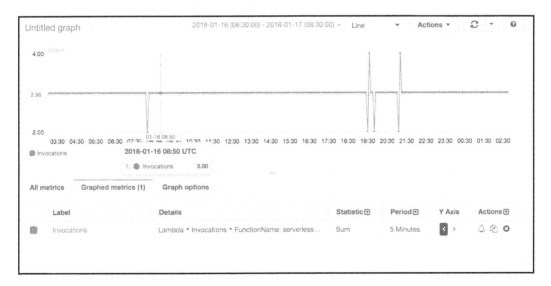

4. The second metric in the Lambda's monitoring dashboard is the **Duration** metric, which tells you the duration of each invocation of our Lambda function. It also has time as the X axis, and the duration time in the Y axis in the unit of milliseconds. It also tells you the maximum, average, and the minimum duration of your Lambda function over a period of time:

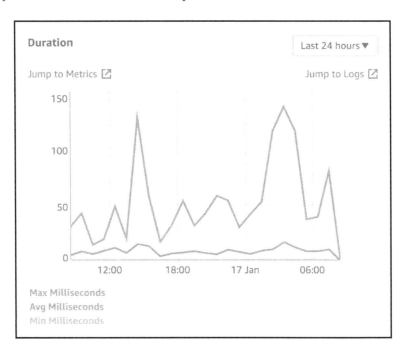

5. Again, clicking on the **Jump to Logs** button will take you to the same page as that of the previous metric. Clicking on the **Jump to Metrics** button will take you to the CloudWatch metric page of the **Duration** metric, which looks like this:

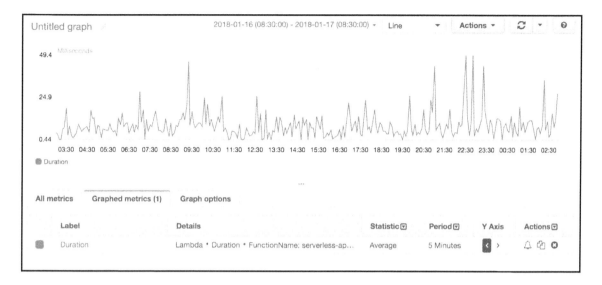

6. The third metric is the **Errors** metric, which helps us keep a look out for errors in our invocations of the Lambda function. The *Y* axis is the number of errors while the *X* axis is the timeline:

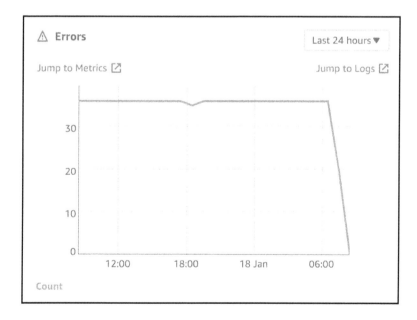

7. The CloudWatch Dashboard of the same metric can be seen by clicking on the **Jump to Metrics** link:

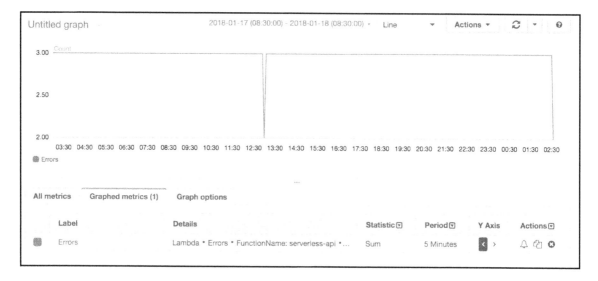

8. The fourth metric is **Throttles**. This metric counts the number of times your Lambda functions have been throttled, which means the number of times the concurrent executions of the functions have breached the set limit of 1,000 per region. We won't encounter this metric very frequently as the Lambda functions which we build as examples in this book stay well within the concurrency limits:

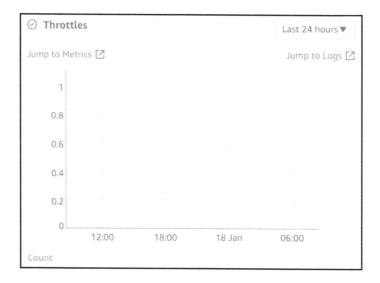

9. By clicking on the **Jump to Metrics** link, we can also see this metric in our CloudWatch Metrics dashboard:

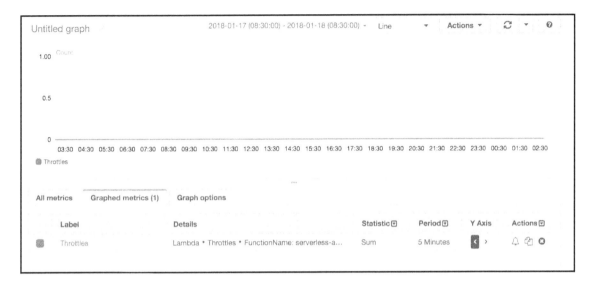

10. The fifth metric is the iterator age. This is only valid for functions which are triggered by the DynamoDB stream or the Kinesis stream. It gives the age of the last record which is processed by the function:

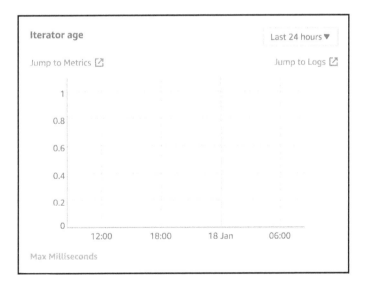

The **Jump to Metrics** link takes you to the CloudWatch Metrics dashboard of this metric:

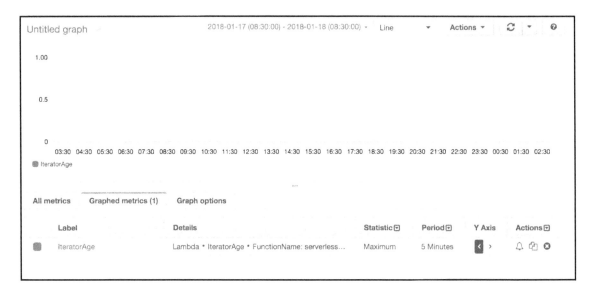

11. The sixth and the last metric is the **DLQ errors** metric. This gives the number of errors that occurred while sending messages (failed event payloads) to a dead letter queue. Most often the errors would be caused due to faulty permission configurations and timeouts:

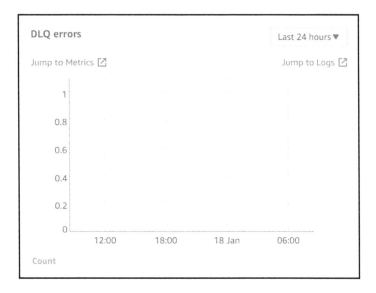

The **Jump to Metrics** link will take you to the CloudWatch Metrics dashboard of the same metric:

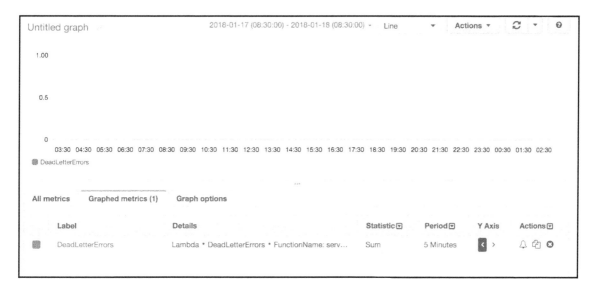

Lambda's logs in CloudWatch

So far, we have learned about and understood the metrics of AWS Lambda in great detail. Now, we will move on to understanding the logs of the Lambda functions. As always, we will try to understand them via the following steps:

1. Logs for AWS Lambda functions are stored in CloudWatch's Logs service. You can access the CloudWatch Logs service by going to the **Logs** dashboard by clicking on the main **CloudWatch** dashboard.

2. When you click on the logs of the **serverless-api**, **/aws/lambda/serverless-api**, in the list, we go to the log stream of the serverless API, which looks like this:

3. Each log stream here is a Lambda invocation. So, whenever your Lambda function is invoked, it creates a new log stream here. If the invocation is a part of Lambda's retry process, then the logs for that particular invocation will be written under the most recent log stream. A single log stream can contain several details. But firstly, let us look at what a particular log stream looks like:

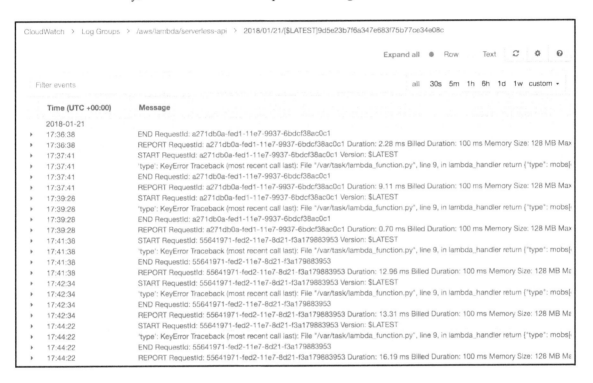

4. Also, if you look closely, you can observe that Lambda's logs also give out information about the duration of the Lambda function's invocation, the duration for which it is billed for, and also the memory used by the function. These metrics help in understanding our functions' performance better and for further optimization and fine tuning:

5. There are several columns in CloudWatch Logs for you to select from, which are not shown in the preceding screenshots. These are the available options:

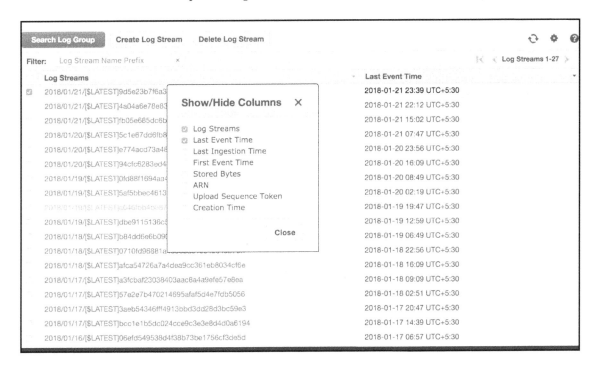

So, when you select more of those, you will see them in your dashboard as columns. These come in handy when you're doing a much more fine-grained debugging of our Lambda functions:

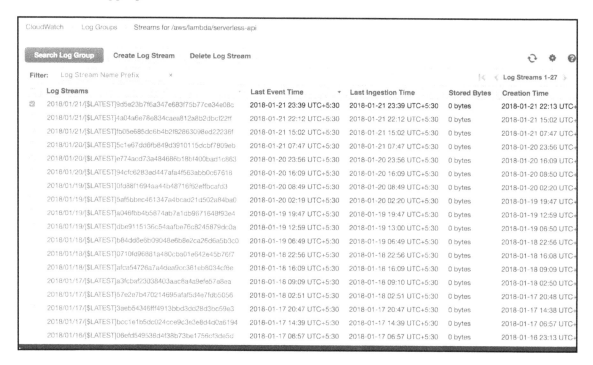

Logging statements in Lambda

Logging your comments and errors clearly is always a good software practice. So, we shall now understand how to log from inside of Lambda functions. There are broadly two ways of logging inside Lambda functions. We shall now learn and understand them via examples from the following steps:

1. The first way is to use Python's `logging` library. This is widely used as a standard practice for logging in Python scripts. We shall edit the code we have written previously for the serverless API and add in the logging statements in it. The code will look like this:

The code which is in the preceding screenshot is as follows:

```python
import logging
logger = logging.getLogger()
logger.setLevel(logging.INFO)
def lambda_handler(event, context):
 mobs = {
 "Sea": ["GoldFish", "Turtle", "Tortoise", "Dolphin", "Seal"],
 "Land": ["Labrador", "Cat", "Dalmatian", "German Shepherd",
 "Beagle", "Golden Retriever"],
 "Exotic": ["Iguana", "Rock Python"]
 }

 logger.info('got event{}'.format(event))
 logger.error('something went wrong')

 return 'Hello from Lambda!'
 #return {"type": mobs[event['type']]}
```

2. Now, when you run the Lambda function after saving, you can see a successful execution statement in green color, which looks like this:

3. When you click on the **Details** option, you can see the logging statements being executed clearly:

4. The next way of logging statements is by simply using the `print` statements in Python. It is the most common way of printing out logging statements in Python scripts. So, we shall add a `Hello from Lambda` print statement in our function code and see if we get the logs in our Lambda execution or not:

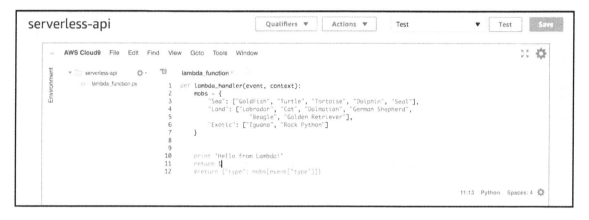

The code for this Lambda function is as follows:

```python
def lambda_handler(event, context):
mobs = {
    "Sea": ["GoldFish", "Turtle", "Tortoise", "Dolphin", "Seal"],
    "Land": ["Labrador", "Cat", "Dalmatian", "German Shepherd",
    "Beagle", "Golden Retriever"],
    "Exotic": ["Iguana", "Rock Python"]
}
print 'Hello from Lambda!'
return 1
#return {"type": mobs[event['type']]}
```

5. When we click on **Test** for executing the code, we should see a green color message, which indicates a successful execution:

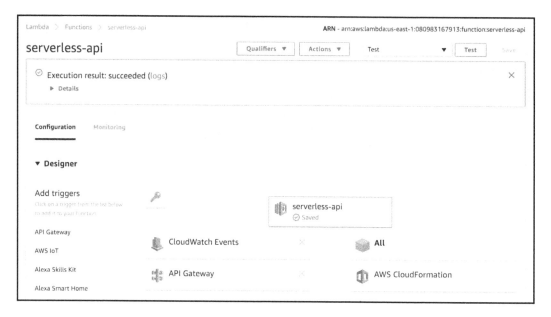

6. Again, just like we did previously, clicking on the **Details** toggle will give you the complete execution logs:

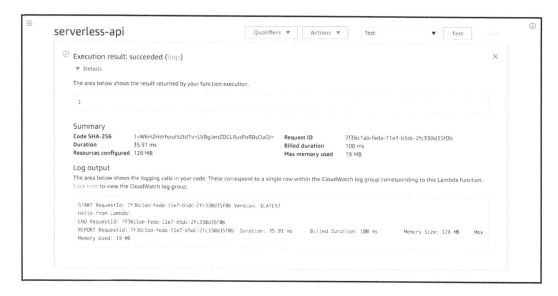

7. We can see the `Hello from Lambda` message too. Out of the two available logging options for our Lambda functions, it is always preferable to use the first option which is via the Python's logging module. This is because that module gives greater flexibility and helps you differentiate between info, error, and debug logs.

Summary

In this chapter, we have learned about the monitoring and the logging capabilities of AWS. We also learned about the available monitoring and logging tools inside the AWS environment. We have also learned how to monitor our Lambda functions and how to set up logging for our Lambda functions.

We have learned about the logging and monitoring practices that are followed by the industry and the various ways one can log statements in Python from inside of a Lambda function.

In the next chapter, we will learn how to scale up our serverless architectures to become distributed and to be able to handle massive workloads while still preserving the positives of a serverless setup.

6
Scaling Up Serverless Architectures

So far, we have learned how to build, monitor, and log serverless functions. In this chapter, we will be learning concepts and engineering techniques that will help scale up serverless applications to be distributed, and that will also enable them to handle heavy workloads with high standards of security and throughput. In this chapter, we will also use some third-party tools, such as Ansible, to scale up our Lambda functions. We will be scaling up our Lambda functions to spawn a distributed serverless architecture, which will involve spawning multiple servers (or instances in the AWS environment). You therefore need to keep that in mind while following the examples mentioned in this chapter.

This chapter assumes a working knowledge of a provisioning tool, such as **Ansible**, **Chef**, and so on. You can quickly read up on or refresh your knowledge of these on their respective sites, where they have quick tutorials. If not, then you can safely skip this chapter and move on to the next.

This chapter consists of five sections, which cover all of the basics of scaling up serverless architectures and will set you up for building bigger, complex serverless architectures:

- Third-party orchestration tools
- The creation and termination of servers
- Security best practices
- Difficulties of scaling up
- Handling difficulties

Third-party orchestration tools

In this section, we will learn and become versed in the concept of infrastructure provisioning and orchestration. We will be exploring a couple of tools, namely Chef and Ansible. Let's get started by following these steps:

1. We will begin with getting introduced to Chef. You can visit the official website of Chef at `https://www.chef.io/chef/`:

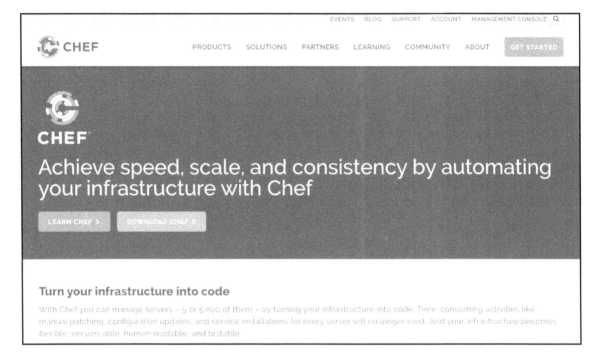

2. Chef has a very good set of tutorials for getting your hands dirty. These are organized in the form of mini 10 to 15 minute tutorials for easy consumption. Head over to `https://learn.chef.io/` to access them:

3. For getting started with infrastructure provisioning and orchestrating, you can refer to the Chef documentation here: `https://docs.chef.io/`. The page looks like this:

4. You can refer to the **AWS Driver Resources** page in the documentation to understand how to interact with various AWS services via Chef at: `https://docs.chef.io/provisioning_aws.html`. The page looks like this:

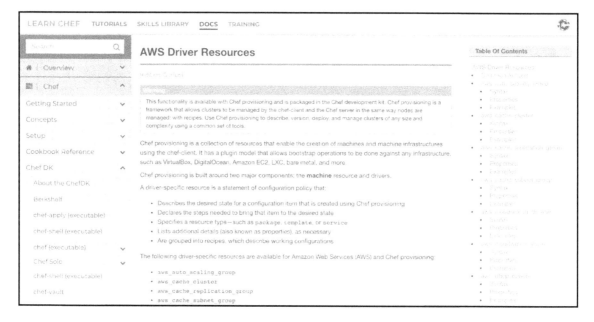

5. You can also refer to the **aws Cookbook** for the same purpose, too. This resource has very good documentation and APIs for interacting with several AWS services. The URL of this documentation is `https://supermarket.chef.io/cookbooks/aws`. The page looks like this:

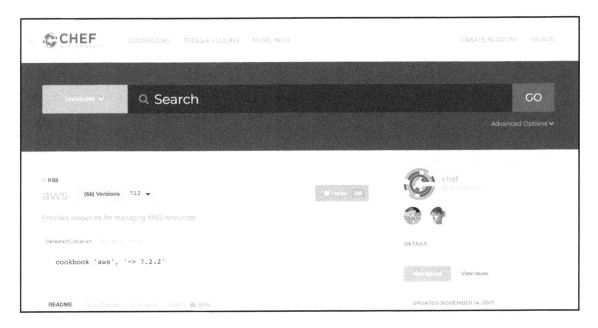

6. A detailed description of the cookbook can be seen when you scroll down, directly after the title of the cookbook:

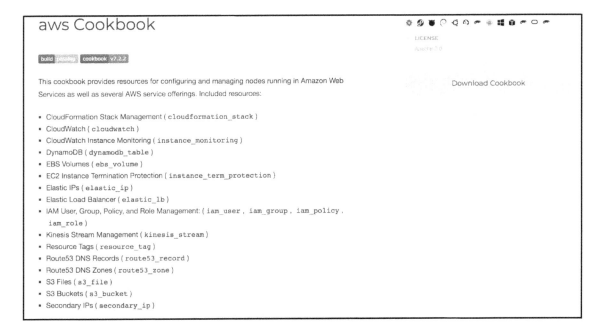

7. One other good tool for provisioning and orchestrating software resources is Ansible. This helps software engineers write code for automating several parts of their infrastructure via *yaml scripts*. Similar to the Chef environment, these scripts are called **cookbooks**.

8. We will be using this tool for learning how to provision our infrastructure in the subsequent sections. The documentation for Ansible can be found at `http://docs.ansible.com/`:

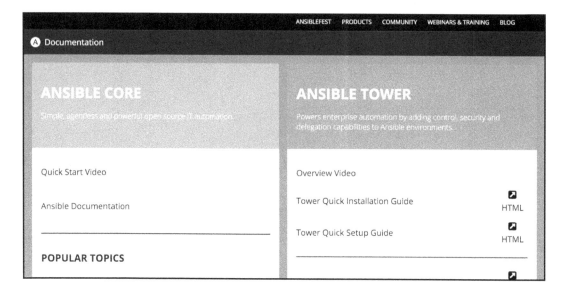

9. The product, **ANSIBLE TOWER**, is out of scope for this book. We will be learning and be working with **ANSIBLE CORE**, which is the flagship product of Ansible and its parent company, Red Hat.

10. Ansible has a very helpful video for helping you better understand and make sense of the tool. It can be accessed when you click on the **Quick Start Video** link in the documentation page:

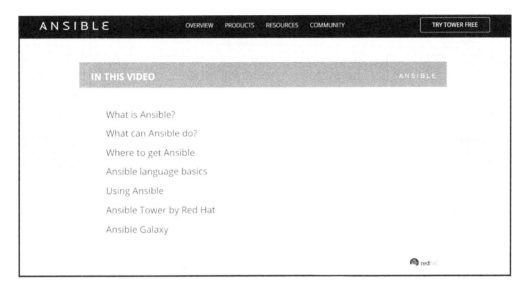

11. After watching the video, you can proceed to understand the product from the documentation itself. The complete documentation of Ansible can be accessed at: `http://docs.ansible.com/ansible/latest/index.html`:

12. The EC2 module is the one we will be using for provisioning and orchestrating our AWS EC2 instances. This part of the documentation has a very clear explanation and demonstration of starting up and terminating EC2 instances, along with adding and mounting volumes; it also enables us to provision our EC2 instances into our own specific **Virtual Private Cloud** (**VPC**) and/or in our own **Security Groups** (**SGs**). The EC2 documentation screen looks like this:

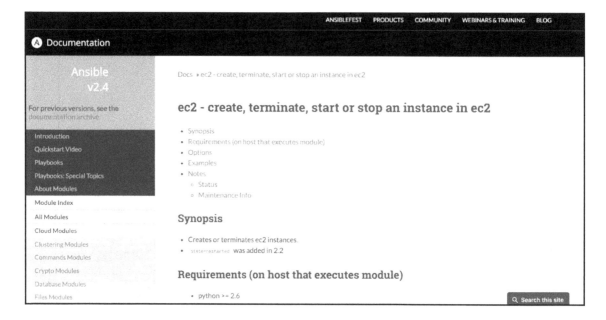

13. You can find this at the following URL of Ansible Core's documentation: `http://docs.ansible.com/ansible/latest/ec2_module.html`. When you scroll down further, you can see several examples of how to use the EC2 module of Ansible for various tasks concerning AWS EC2 instances. Some of them can be seen as follows:

Examples

```
# Note: These examples do not set authentication details, see the AWS Guide for details.

# Basic provisioning example
- ec2:
    key_name: mykey
    instance_type: t2.micro
    image: ami-123456
    wait: yes
    group: webserver
    count: 3
    vpc_subnet_id: subnet-29e63245
    assign_public_ip: yes

# Advanced example with tagging and CloudWatch
- ec2:
    key_name: mykey
    group: databases
    instance_type: t2.micro
    image: ami-123456
    wait: yes
    wait_timeout: 500
    count: 5
    instance_tags:
       db: postgres
    monitoring: yes
    vpc_subnet_id: subnet-29e63245
    assign_public_ip: yes

# Single instance with additional IOPS volume from snapshot and volume delete on termination
- ec2:
    key_name: mykey
    group: webserver
```

Q Search this site

The creation and termination of servers

In this chapter, we will learn how to use some third-party tools that will help us in building the required architecture. Like all of the sections in this chapter, the information will be broken down into steps:

1. The first tool we will be learning about is Ansible. It is a provisioning and orchestrating tool, that helps in automating several parts of an infrastructure. Depending on when you are reading this book, the Ansible project's homepage (`https://www.ansible.com/`) will look something like this:

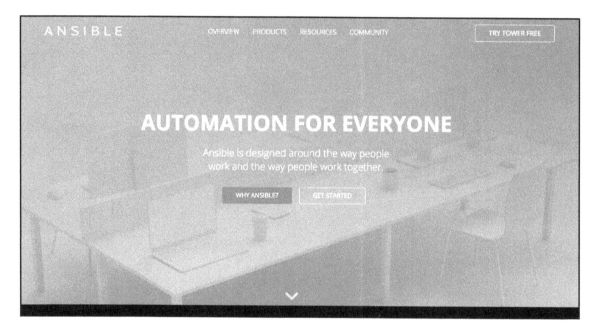

2. The installation process for Ansible is different for different operating systems. The instructions for some popular operating systems are as follows:

   - **For Ubuntu**:

     ```
     sudo apt-get update
     sudo apt-get install software-properties-common
     sudo apt-add-repository ppa:ansible/ansible
     sudo apt-get update
     sudo apt-get install ansible
     ```

- **For Linux**:

```
git clone https://github.com/ansible/ansible.git
cd ./ansible
make rpm
sudo rpm -Uvh ./rpm-build/ansible-*.noarch.rpm
```

- **For OS X**:

```
sudo pip install ansible
```

3. Now, we will understand the concept of **nohup**. So, you don't need to have a persistent SSH connection to the server for making a `nohup` command run, therefore we will be using this technique for running our master–server architecture (to know more about nohup refer to: `https://en.wikipedia.org/wiki/Nohup`).

 Let's look at its definition on Wikipedia (from the time of writing this book), **nohup** is a POSIX command to ignore the HUP (hangup) signal. The HUP signal is, by convention, the way a terminal warns dependent processes of logout.

4. We will now learn how to provision servers from Ansible, SSH into them, run a simple `apt-get update` task in them, and terminate them. From this, you will learn how to write Ansible scripts, as well as understand how Ansible handles the provisioning of cloud resources. The following Ansible script will help you understand how to provision an EC2 instance:

```
- hosts: localhost
  connection: local
  remote_user: test
  gather_facts: no

  environment:
    AWS_ACCESS_KEY_ID: "{{ aws_id }}"
    AWS_SECRET_ACCESS_KEY: "{{ aws_key }}"

    AWS_DEFAULT_REGION: "{{ aws_region }}"

  tasks:
- name: Provisioning EC2 instaces
  ec2:
    assign_public_ip: no
    aws_access_key: "{{ access_key }}"
    aws_secret_key: "{{ secret_key }}"
```

```
region: "{{ aws_region }}"
image: "{{ image_instance }}"
instance_type: "{{ instance_type }}"
key_name: "{{ ssh_keyname }}"
state: present
group_id: "{{ security_group }}"
vpc_subnet_id: "{{ subnet }}"
instance_profile_name: "{{ Profile_Name }}"
wait: true
instance_tags:
   Name: "{{ Instance_Name }}"
delete_on_termination: yes
register: ec2
ignore_errors: True
```

The values in the `{{ }}` brackets need to be filled in as per your convenience and specifications. The preceding code will create an EC2 instance in your console and name it, as per the specification which is given in the `{{ Instance_Name }}` section.

5. The `ansible.cfg` file should include all of the details which give instructions about the control path, the details regarding the forwarding agent, and also the path to the EC2 instance key. The `ansible.cfg` file should look like this:

```
[ssh_connection]
ssh_args=-o ControlMaster=auto -o ControlPersist=60s -o
ControlPath=/tmp/ansible-ssh-%h-%p-%r -o ForwardAgent=yes

[defaults]
private_key_file=/path/to/key/key.pem
```

6. When you execute this code using `ansible-playbook -vvv < name-of-playbook >.yml`, you can see the EC2 instance being created in your EC2 console:

7. Now, we will terminate the instance which we have just created via Ansible. This will also be done in an Ansible script, similar to how we provisioned the instance. The following code does this:

```
tasks:
  - name: Terminate instances that were previously launched
    connection: local
    become: false
    ec2:
      state: 'absent'
      instance_ids: '{{ ec2.instance_ids }}'
      region: '{{ aws_region }}'
    register: TerminateWorker
    ignore_errors: True
```

8. So, now you can see the instance being terminated in the console. Note that the code is the same up until the tasks, such as provisioning and terminating instances, so you can copy and paste from the provisioning task:

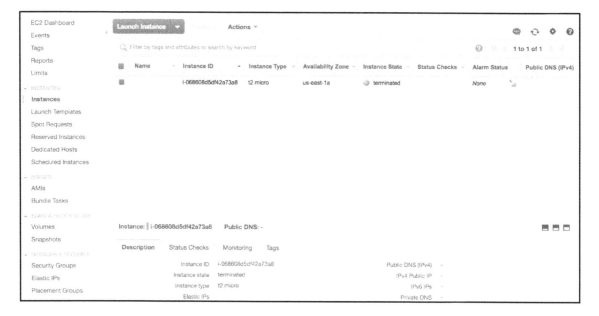

So, we have successfully learned how to provision and terminate EC2 instances via an Ansible script. We will use this knowledge for provisioning and will be terminating EC2 instances at the same time.

9. Making a small change to the provisioning code in the yaml script we used previously, we can provision multiple servers (EC2 instances) at the same time, by simply adding the count parameter. The following code will provision the number of instances mentioned in the *jinja template*, beside the count parameter. In our example, it is ninstances:

```
- hosts: localhost
  connection: local
  remote_user: test
  gather_facts: no


  environment:
    AWS_ACCESS_KEY_ID: "{{ aws_id }}"
    AWS_SECRET_ACCESS_KEY: "{{ aws_key }}"
```

```
            AWS_DEFAULT_REGION: "{{ aws_region }}"

       tasks:
     - name: Provisioning EC2 instaces
       ec2:
         assign_public_ip: no
         aws_access_key: "{{ access_key }}"
         aws_secret_key: "{{ secret_key }}"
         region: "{{ aws_region }}"
         image: "{{ image_instance }}"
         instance_type: "{{ instance_type }}"
         key_name: "{{ ssh_keyname }}"
         count: "{{ ninstances }}"
         state: present
         group_id: "{{ security_group }}"
         vpc_subnet_id: "{{ subnet }}"
         instance_profile_name: "{{ Profile_Name }}"
         wait: true
         instance_tags:
           Name: "{{ Instance_Name }}"
         delete_on_termination: yes
         register: ec2
```

10. Now, as we have our Ansible script ready, we will now use it to start our infrastructure from the Lambda function. For that, we will make use of our knowledge of nohup.

11. In your Lambda function, all you need to do is to write the logic for creating a server, and then do some basic installations using the library, paramiko, and then run the Ansible script in a nohup mode, as shown here:

```
import paramiko
import boto3
import logging

logger = logging.getLogger(__name__)
logger.setLevel(logging.CRITICAL)
region = 'us-east-1'
image = 'ami-<>'
ubuntu_image = 'ami-<>'
keyname = '<>'

def lambda_handler(event, context):
    credentials = {<>}
    k = paramiko.RSAKey.from_private_key_file("<>")
        c = paramiko.SSHClient()
    c.set_missing_host_key_policy(paramiko.AutoAddPolicy())
    logging.critical("Creating Session")
```

```
        session = boto3.Session(credentials['AccessKeyId'],
        credentials['SecretAccessKey'],
        aws_session_token=credentials['SessionToken'],
region_name=region)
        logging.critical("Created Session")
        logging.critical("Create Resource")
        ec2 = session.resource('ec2', region_name=region)
        logging.critical("Created Resource")
        logging.critical("Key Verification")

        key = '<>'
        k = paramiko.RSAKey.from_private_key_file(key)
        c = paramiko.SSHClient()
        c.set_missing_host_key_policy(paramiko.AutoAddPolicy())
        logging.critical("Key Verification done")
        # Generate Presigned URL for downloading EC2 key from       an
S3 bucket into master
        s3client = session.client('s3')

# Presigned url for downloading pem file of the server from an
S3 bucket
        url = s3client.generate_presigned_url('get_object',
Params={'Bucket': '<bucket_name>', 'Key':
'<file_name_of_key>'},
ExpiresIn=300)
        command = 'wget ' + '-O <>.pem ' + "'" + url + "'"
        logging.critical("Create Instance")
while True:
        try:
            logging.critical("Trying")
            c.connect(hostname=dns_name, username="ubuntu", pkey=k)
        except:
            logging.critical("Failed")
        continue
            break
        logging.critical("connected")

        if size == 0:
            s3client.upload_file('<>.pem', '<bucket_name>',
'<>.pem')
        else:
            pass
        set_key = credentials['AccessKeyId']
        set_secret = credentials['SecretAccessKey']
        set_token = credentials['SessionToken']

# Commands to run inside the SSH session of the server
        commands = [command,
```

```
"sudo apt-get -y update",
"sudo apt-add-repository -y ppa:ansible/ansible",
"sudo apt-get -y update",
"sudo apt-get install -y ansible python-pip git awscli",
"sudo pip install boto markupsafe boto3 python-dateutil
futures",
"ssh-keyscan -H github.com >> ~/.ssh/known_hosts",
"git clone <repository where your ansible script is>
/home/ubuntu/<>/",
"chmod 400 <>.pem",
"cd <>/<>/; pwd ; nohup ansible-playbook -vvv provision.yml >
ansible.out 2> ansible.err < /dev/null &"]

# Running the commands
    for command in commands:
        logging.critical("Executing %s", command)
stdin, stdout, stderr = c.exec_command(command)
    logging.critical(stdout.read())
    logging.critical("Errors : %s", stderr.read())
        c.close()
    return dns_name
```

Security best practices

Ensuring high-level security has always been a major problem for microservices. There are multiple levels of software that you need to keep in mind while designing the security layers. The engineers need to define the security protocols for each of the services and then also define the protocols for the data interaction and transfer between each service.

You have to keep all these aspects in mind before architecting distributed serverless systems, where (almost) each Ansible task is a microservice. In this section, we will understand how to architect the security protocols, and also monitor them using some of AWS's built-in services.

We will go through a step-by-step understanding of how to write security protocols for our serverless architectures:

1. Firstly, whenever you are creating a session inside your AWS Python scripts using **Boto**, try to create temporary credentials using the **AWS Secure Token Service** (**STS**), which creates temporary credentials for a specific period of time:

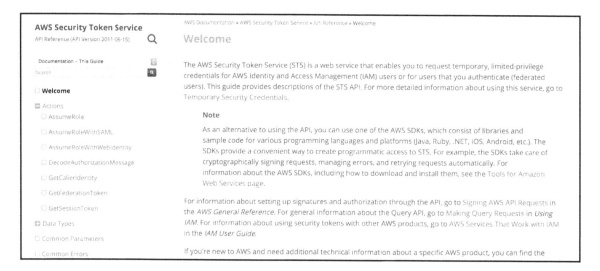

 You can look at the documentation of the STS at: `https://docs.aws.amazon.com/STS/latest/APIReference/Welcome.html`.

2. The **AssumeRole** API of the STS service enables programmers to assumes IAM roles into their code:

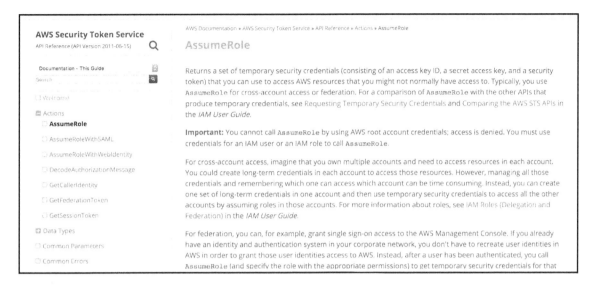

 You can find its documentation on the following page: `https://docs.aws.amazon.com/STS/latest/APIReference/API_AssumeRole.html`

3. The Python version of this can be referred to, in the `boto3` documentation:

This documentation can be found here: `http://boto3.readthedocs.io/en/latest/reference/services/sts.html`.

4. Scrolling down, you can find the usage of the **AssumeRole** API in Python:

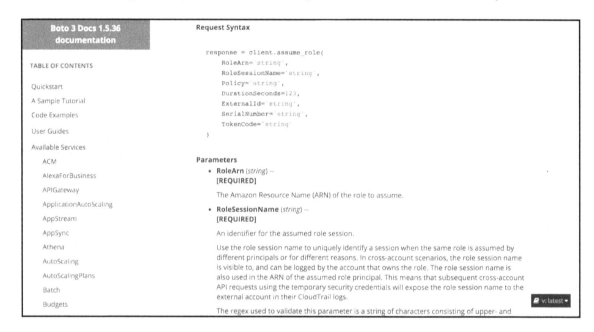

5. Proper care should be taken so that the data exchange between microservices and/or between the microservices and other AWS resources happens securely with authentication. For example, the developer can configure S3 buckets to restrict actions such as unencrypted uploads, downloads, and insecure file transfers. The bucket policy can be written as follows to ensure all of these things are taken care of:

```
{
    "Version": "2012-10-17",
    "Id": "PutObjPolicy",
    "Statement": [
    {
        "Sid": "DenyIncorrectEncryptionHeader",
        "Effect": "Deny",
        "Principal": "*",
        "Action": "s3:PutObject",
        "Resource": "arn:aws:s3:::<bucket_name>/*",
```

```
            "Condition": {
                "StringNotEquals": {
                    "s3:x-amz-server-side-encryption": "aws:kms"
                }
            }
        },
        {
            "Sid": "DenyUnEncryptedObjectUploads",
            "Effect": "Deny",
            "Principal": "*",
            "Action": "s3:PutObject",
            "Resource": "arn:aws:s3:::<bucket_name2>/*",
            "Condition": {
                "Null": {
                    "s3:x-amz-server-side-encryption": "true"
                }
            }
        },
        {
            "Sid": "DenyNonSecureTraffic",
            "Effect": "Deny",
            "Principal": "*",
            "Action": "s3:*",
            "Resource": "arn:aws:s3:::<bucket_name>/*",
            "Condition": {
                "Bool": {
                    "aws:SecureTransport": "false"
                }
            }
        },
        {
            "Sid": "DenyNonSecureTraffic",
            "Effect": "Deny",
            "Principal": "*",
            "Action": "s3:*",
            "Resource": "arn:aws:s3:::<bucket_name2>/*",
            "Condition": {
                "Bool": {
                    "aws:SecureTransport": "false"
                }
            }
        }
    ]
}
```

6. Once you have finished writing the bucket policy, you can update it in the **Bucket Policy** section of S3:

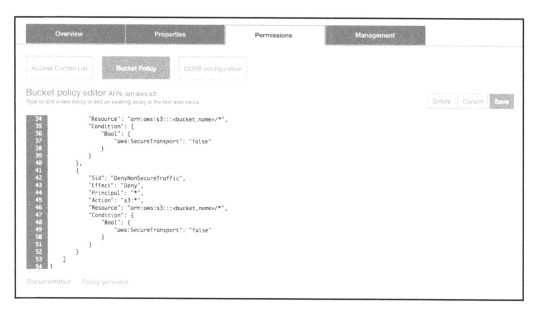

7. **AWS Config** provides a very useful interface for monitoring several security threats and helps in efficiently avoiding or catching them. The dashboard of **AWS Config** looks like this:

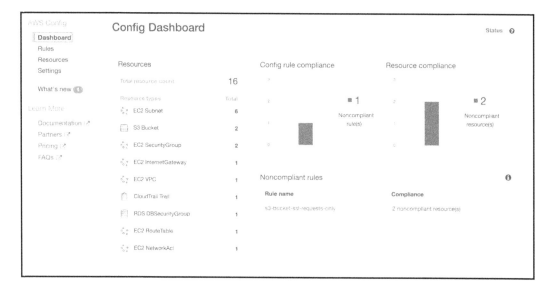

8. You can see that the dashboard shows **2 non-compliant resource(s)** which means that two of my AWS resources are not complying with the rules that I have put into config. Let's have a look at these rules:

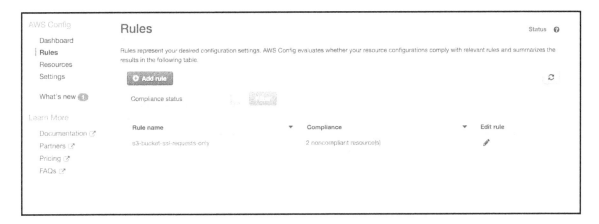

This means that we have two AWS S3 buckets which do not have SSL requests turned on via the bucket policy. Once you click on the **Rules** link, you can see more details which include the bucket(s) names, and also the timestamps at which these configuration changes have been recorded:

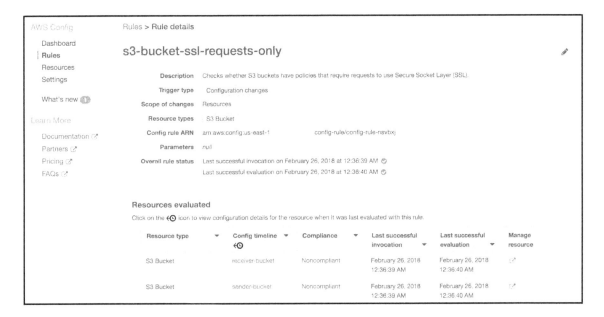

Identifying and handling difficulties in scaling

Scaling up distributed serverless systems comes with its own set of engineering roadblocks and problems, and the fact that the concept of serverless systems is still in a very infantile stage, means that most of those problems are still unsolved. But, that shouldn't stop us from trying to solve and work around these roadblocks.

We will try and understand some of these roadblocks, and also learn how to solve or work around them, as discussed here:

- This is more of an architect's mistake rather than a roadblock. However, it is important to address this as one too many architects/software engineers fell and fall into the overestimation or the underestimation trap. The problem we will try to address is the exact number of instances you have to launch when scaling up. In most self-hosted MapReduce-style systems, it is taken care of out of the box.
- This problem can be taken care of, by properly benchmarking the workloads beforehand on different types of instances, and scale accordingly. Let's understand this by taking an example of a machine learning pipeline. Thanks to our benchmarking efforts, we already know that an *m3.medium* instance can handle 100 files in 10 minutes. So, if my workload has 202 files and I want it to be completed in close to 10 minutes, I would like to have two such instances for handling this. Even if we don't know the workloads in advance, we can write a Python script for getting that number from wherever the data is, be it an SQS queue pointer, or S3, or some other database; and that number can be entered into the Ansible script and make the playbook run.
- As we have already learned about handling security in huge serverless systems, we will keep this short. There are several complex data movements happening inside a large distributed serverless workload. Using proper security protocols and monitoring them, as mentioned in detail in the previous security section, will help in overcoming this problem.
- Logging is a major problem in distributed serverless systems, which is also still unsolved completely. As the systems and containers are destroyed once the workload has been completed, logging has been a very difficult task to undertake. There are several ways you can log the workflow. The most popular ones are logging every Ansible task separately, and one where the last Ansible task is to zip up the logs and send the zipped file to a data store, such as S3 or Logstash. The last one is the most preferred way as it captures the execution flow better, as the entire log trace is in a single file.

- Monitoring is similar to logging. Monitoring these systems is also mostly an unsolved problem. As the servers are all terminated once the workload is run, we can't poll for historic logs from the servers, and latency also will not be tolerated, or more precisely, will not be possible. Monitor every task of Ansible by having a task after each, that sends a custom metric to CloudWatch upon a condition that the previous task has executed successfully or not. This will look something like this:

```
- name: OnDemandProvision on success
  command: aws cloudwatch put-metric-data --metric-name OnDemandProvision[M] --namespace Ansible --value 1
  when: ec2|succeeded
- name: OnDemandProvision on failure
  command: aws cloudwatch put-metric-data --metric-name OnDemandProvision[M] --namespace Ansible --value 0
  when: ec2|failed
```

- Debugging trial runs can also become very frustrating, very fast. This is because, if you are not quick, the entire system can be terminated before you even get a chance to look at the logs. Also, Ansible emits very verbose logs while debugging, which might seem overwhelming when spawning several instances.
- Some basic Unix hacks can help in handling these problems. The most important one is to monitor the tail of the log file, about 50 lines or so. This helps in not getting overwhelmed by the huge amount of logs, and it also keeps an eye on the execution of the Ansible notebook.

Summary

In this chapter, we have learned how to scale up our serverless architecture(s) to being massively distributed serverless infrastructure(s). We have learned how to build on our existing knowledge of building and deploying Lambda infrastructures to handle massive workloads.

We have learned to use the concept of nohup to use our Lambda function as a launch board for building a master-worker architecture that takes parallel computing into account. We have learned how to leverage configuration and orchestration tools, such as Ansible and Chef, to spawn and orchestrate multiple EC2 instances.

The knowledge gained from this chapter will open doors for building many complex infrastructures which can handle data and requests, both in terms of size and speed. This will allow you to operate multiple microservices closely intertwined together. This will also help you to build MapReduce-style systems and interact with other AWS services, seamlessly.

Security in AWS Lambda 7

We have learned how to build and configure serverless functions in AWS Lambda. We have learned how to scale them up using third-party tools. We have also had a close look at how microservices work and how to ensure security in them, while ensuring resilience and speed.

In this chapter, we will understand security in the AWS environment, keeping in mind our Lambda functions. We will understand how services, such as AWS VPCs, security groups, and subnets work, with respect to Lambda functions.

This chapter covers the following topics:

- Understanding AWS VPCs
- Understanding subnets in VPCs
- Securing Lambda inside private subnets
- Controlling access to Lambda functions
- Using STS inside Lambda for secure session-based execution

Understanding AWS Virtual Private Clouds (VPCs)

In this section, we will understand AWS VPCs. **VPCs** are a very common component in the security layers of the AWS environment; they are isolated parts of the cloud where users can host their services and build their infrastructures. VPCs are the first layer of security. We will try to understand VPCs in the context of Lambda functions, in the form of bullet points, given here:

1. VPCs can be created and modified in the AWS's VPC service dashboard, which looks like this:

2. Now, let's quickly learn how to create a VPC of our own. For that, click on **Create VPC**. You will see a pop-up box which asks you to enter more meta information for your new VPC:

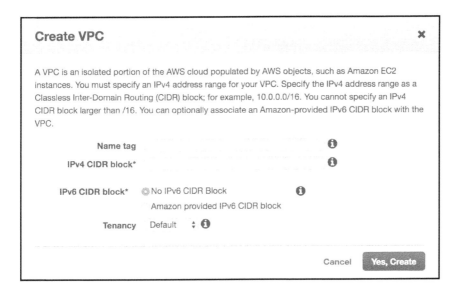

3. The **Name tag** box needs to have the name of the VPC. The **IPv4 CIDR block** is where you enter your IP range for classless inter-domain routing. Then, you can choose whether you want an IPv6 CIDR block or not. You can also select the **Tenancy** settings; this defines how your EC2 instances run within your VPC, and the resource sharing accordingly:

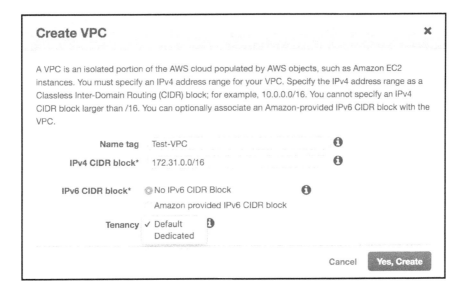

4. We have successfully created our VPC with the necessary settings and with the `Test-VPC` name. We can see this in our dashboard with all the corresponding meta settings:

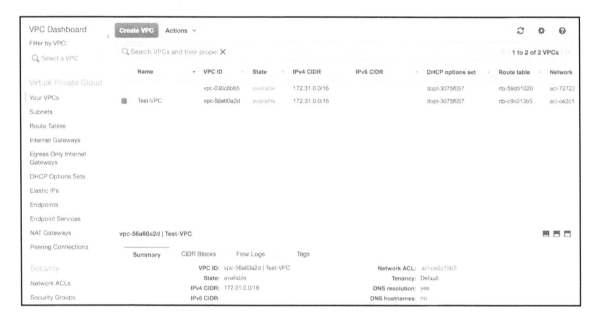

5. You can also see a summary of the VPC which includes the IPv4 settings, the **Network Access Control List** (**ACL**) settings, the **Dynamic Host Configuration Protocol** (**DHCP**) options, and also the DNS settings, all of which can also be configured later according to our needs. You can also see IPv4 CIDR blocks under the next **CIDR Blocks** tab:

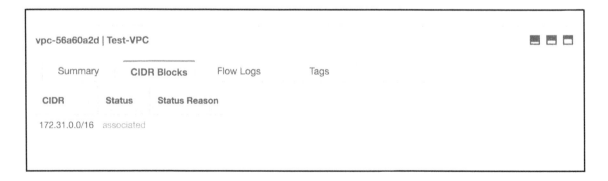

6. We can also create VPC flow logs, which log traffic and data movements in and out of the VPC. This will promote better log management, ensuring security, and better monitoring. Currently, flow logs have not been set up:

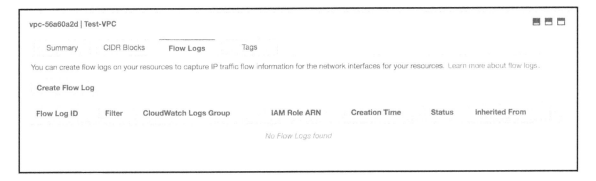

7. To create VPC flow logs, you can just click on the **Create Flow Log** button at the bottom. This will open up a flow log creation wizard where you can enter the details for the various settings, accordingly. The creation wizard looks like this:

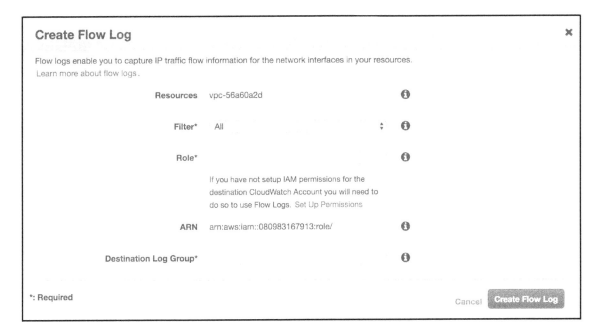

8. Once all the details have been entered, you can go ahead and click on the **Create Flow Log** option at the bottom, which will create the VPC flow log with the desired settings:

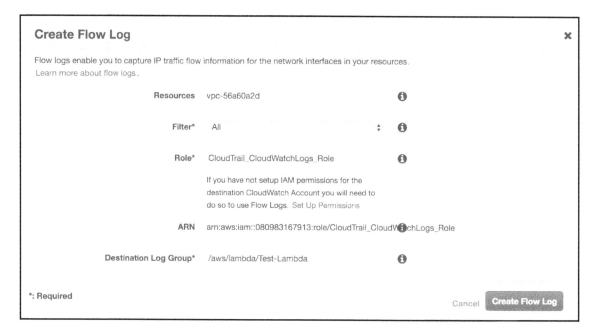

9. Once created, you can see the newly created VPC flow log under the **Flow Logs** tab, as shown here:

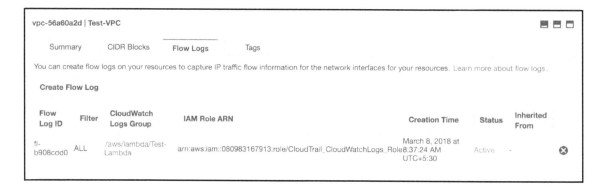

10. Now, let's understand VPCs from AWS Lambda's point of view. Just like any other AWS resource, Lambda functions can also be hosted inside VPCs. You can see that setting under the **Network** section of your AWS Lambda function. It looks like this:

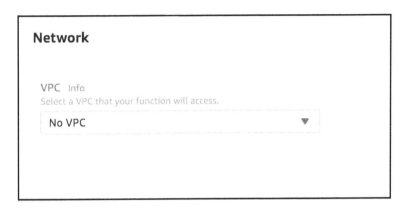

11. From the drop-down list, you can select a VPC in which you want to host your Lambda function:

12. Once you select a VPC, it will further ask you for details regarding subnets, security groups, and so on, as shown in the following screenshot. We will learn about them in the sections following this, so, we will configure the VPC for our Lambda function later:

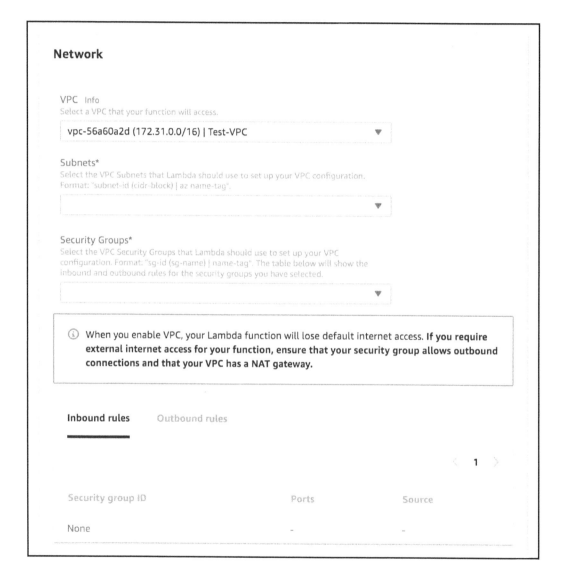

Understanding subnets in VPCs

In this section, we will learn about and understand AWS subnets, which are subparts of AWS VPCs. VPCs can be further divided into multiple subnets. These subnets can either be public or private, depending on the security needs of your architecture. We will look at the concept of subnets from the point of view of AWS Lambda functions.

We will perform the following steps:

1. You can go to the **Subnets** menu via the VPC page itself. You need to click on the **Subnets** option under the **Your VPCs** option on the left:

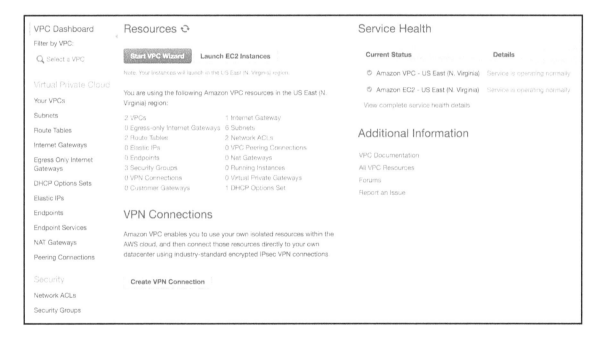

2. This will take you to the subnets console, where you will see some already existing subnets. These are the default subnets for each availability zone in your region:

3. Now, to create a new subnet, you need to click on the blue **Create Subnet** button on the top-left side of the console. In the creation wizard, you will be asked to enter the following details—the name of the subnet, the VPC you want to place it in, availability zones, and also preferred IPv4 CIDR blocks. I have placed this subnet inside the VPC we created in the previous section:

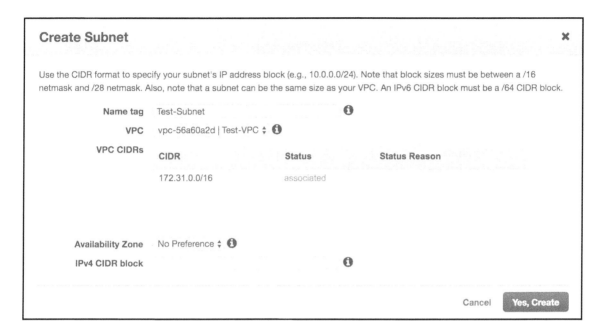

4. When you click on the **Yes, Create** button on the bottom-right side of the creation wizard, the new subnet is created. You can see it listed in the list of your subnets on your console:

5. Now, we will fill in the security settings for our Lambda function with our VPC and subnets, which we have just created. Currently, this is what the **Network** setting for AWS Lambda looks like:

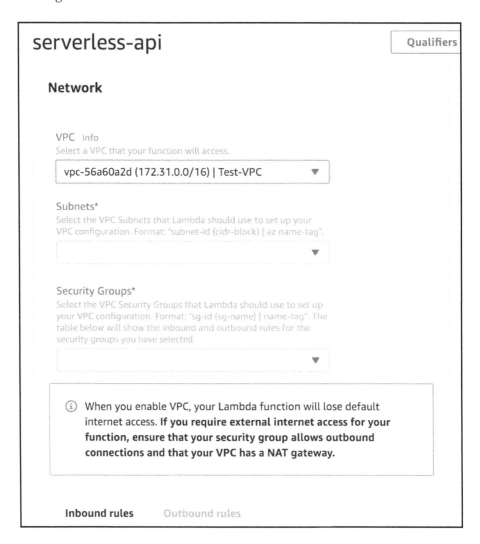

6. After adding in the required settings, which are the details of the VPC, subnet and security groups, the **Network** settings of our Lambda function will look like this:

...

7. After setting up your network settings for your Lambda function, click on the orange **Save** button on the top-right of your Lambda console to save those settings to your Lambda function.

Securing Lambda inside private subnets

Private subnets are subnets that are not open to the internet. All of their traffic is routed via the public subnet in the same VPC using the concept of route tables. Let's understand how to position our Lambda functions inside private subnets to add an extra layer of security:

1. Subnets created in the AWS console are not private by default. Let's evaluate and confirm this by going through the details of the subnet that we just created:

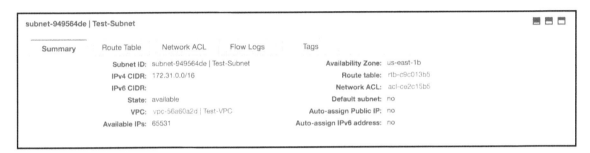

2. Clicking on the **Route Table** tab will show us the routing settings of our subnet, which basically tells us what kind of traffic is allowed into it:

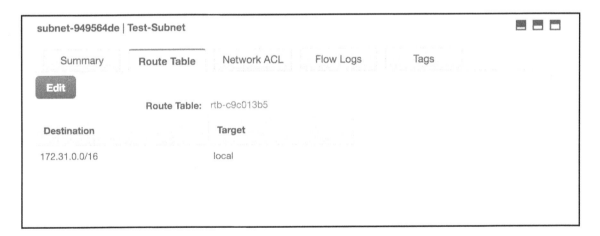

3. In the **Network ACL** tab, you can see the network rules assigned for our subnet. Here, we can see that the subnet is open to all traffic (**0.0.0.0/0**). So, in order to make our subnet private, we need to fix this:

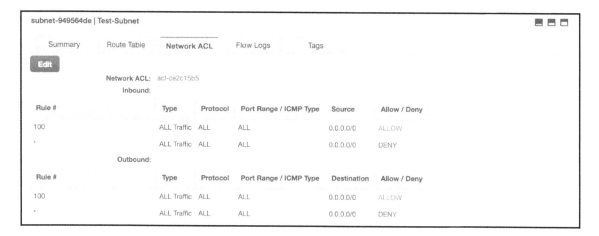

4. Go to the **Network ACLs** console by clicking on the link to the left side of your console. You will arrive at the following page:

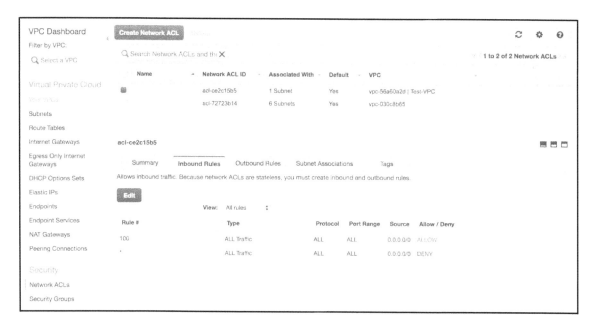

5. Now, click on the blue **Create Network ACL** button to create a new ACL. Select our VPC and then enter a name for the ACL in the creation wizard:

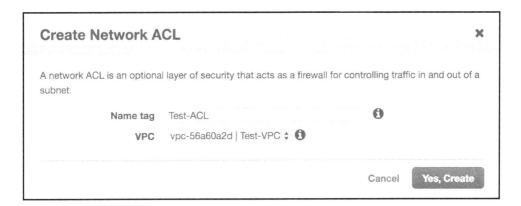

6. Now, in the inbound rules of the new ACL, add in the following rule. In the **Source** section, add the IPv4 setting of any of your public subnets and click **Save**:

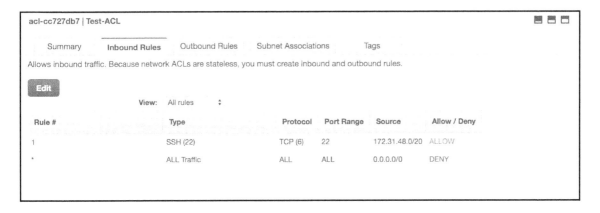

7. Now, replace the ACL of our current subnet with the new one that will make our subnet a private subnet:

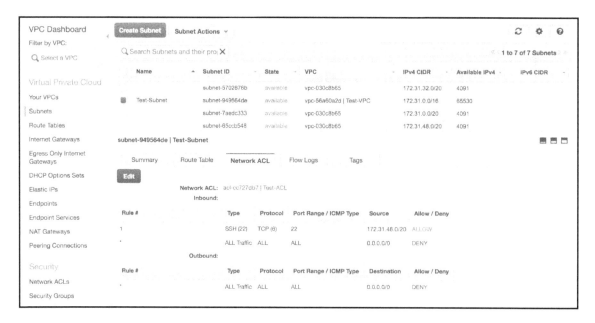

Now, we have our Lambda function in a private subnet, making it more secure.

Controlling access to Lambda functions

We have gone through all the security settings needed to ensure that our Lambda functions and our serverless architectures are secure. So, an engineer working on serverless systems should keep the following points in mind while designing their infrastructure from a security point of view:

- The VPC and the subnet settings can be added under the **Network** section of the Lambda function.
- It is recommended that the Lambda function is placed across at least two subnets for fault tolerance purposes. However, this is not compulsory.
- If you are placing your Lambda function inside a private subnet, you need to ensure that the private subnet is receiving the appropriate traffic from your public subnet(s) in that VPC. If not, then the Lambda function is essentially locked out.

Using STS inside Lambda for secure session-based execution

While accessing other AWS services and components from inside your Lambda functions, you can make use of **AWS's Simple Token Service (STS)** to ensure session-based access, which will essentially add an extra layer of security. As we have already discussed, and learned how to use, STS credentials in our code, we will skip over to the documentation links.

The official documentation of AWS STS will help you understand how session-based access works: `https://docs.aws.amazon.com/IAM/latest/UserGuide/id_credentials_temp.html`.

And this is the *Boto3 Python Documentation* for using STS credentials inside Python code: `http://boto3.readthedocs.io/en/latest/reference/services/sts.html`.

Summary

In this chapter, we have learned how security works in Lambda functions in a deep-dive mode. We have understood how VPCs and subnets work in the AWS environment. We have learned to create a VPC and also created public and private subnets. This will give you a better understanding of how security works from the whole of the AWS perspective.

We have also learned how to place your Lambda functions inside the VPCs and the subnets we have created throughout this chapter. We understood how to handle and route traffic inside our VPCs and subnets.

Finally, we also learned how to implement better security in our Python code using session-based access to other AWS components, thereby placing security in the control of the developer.

In the next chapter, you will learn about the **Serverless Application Model (SAM)** and how to write SAM models and deploy your Lambda applications through them.

8
Deploying a Lambda Function with SAM

So far, we have learned about Lambda functions and how to build them. We have learned that a Lambda function has a definite set of triggers that would trigger the function to carry out a particular task. The task is written as a Python module and the script is what we call a function. We have also learned about the different settings of Lambda functions, which include its core settings and also other settings, such as security and network.

There is also another alternative to creating and deploying Lambda functions, which is the **AWS Serverless Application Model** (**AWS SAM**). This format is based on the concept of **infrastructure as code**. This concept is inspired by **AWS CloudFormation**, which is a form of infrastructure as code.

We will be learning about AWS CloudFormation and using that knowledge to understand and build AWS SAM models for creating Lambda functions. We will be covering the following concepts in this chapter:

- Deploying Lambda functions
- Using CloudFormation for serverless services
- Deploying with SAM
- Understanding security in SAM

Introduction to SAM

In this section, we will learn about SAM, which will help us build and deploy serverless functions:

1. As mentioned earlier, SAM is about writing infrastructure as code. So, this is what a Lambda function would be described as in SAM:

```
AWSTemplateFormatVersion: '2010-09-09'
Transform: AWS::Serverless-2016-10-31
Resources:
    < Name of function >:
        Type: AWS::Serverless::Function
        Properties:
            Handler: < index.handler >
            Runtime: < runtime >
            CodeUri: < URI of the bucket >
```

2. In this block of code, we enter the details—the name of the function, and the URI of the S3 bucket where our code package is hosted. In the same way that we named the index and the handler in our Lambda settings, we need to enter those details here, too. The `index.handler` is the file in which our function code is located. The `Handler` is the name of the function in which our Lambda logic is written. Also, the `Runtime` is user-defined. You can select from all the available languages that are supported by AWS Lambda. The scope of this book is limited to the Python language, so we will stick to either of the available Python versions:

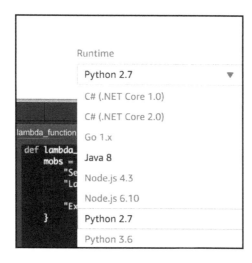

3. We can also add environment variables, as shown here, in our Lambda function, too. These can be very easily edited and configured just as we add, update, and/or delete code, which is an added advantage of the infrastructure as code style of building infrastructures:

```
AWSTemplateFormatVersion: '2010-09-09'
Transform: AWS::Serverless-2016-10-31
Resources:
    PutFunction:
        Type: AWS::Serverless::Function
        Properties:
            Handler: index.handler
            Runtime: < runtime >
            Policies: < AWSLambdaDynamoDBExecutionRole >
            CodeUri: < URI of the zipped function package >
            Environment:
                Variables:
                    TABLE_NAME: !Ref Table
DeleteFunction:
    Type: AWS::Serverless::Function
     Properties:
        Handler: index.handler
        Runtime: nodejs6.10
        Policies: AWSLambdaDynamoDBExecutionRole
         CodeUri: s3://bucketName/codepackage.zip
        Environment:
            Variables:
                TABLE_NAME: !Ref Table
        Events:
            Stream:
                Type: DynamoDB
                Properties:
                    Stream: !GetAtt DynamoDBTable.StreamArn
                    BatchSize: 100
                    StartingPosition: TRIM_HORIZON
DynamoDBTable:
    Type: AWS::DynamoDB::Table
    Properties:
        AttributeDefinitions:
            - AttributeName: id
                AttributeType: S
        KeySchema:
            - AttributeName: id
                KeyType: HASH
        ProvisionedThroughput:
            ReadCapacityUnits: 5
            WriteCapacityUnits: 5
```

```
      StreamSpecification:
          StreamViewType: streamview type
```

4. The preceding SAM code invokes two Lambda functions that point to an AWS `DynamoDB` table. The entire SAM code is an application that consists of a couple of Lambda functions. You need to enter the necessary details for making this work. The `Runtime` needs to be updated with either of the available Python runtimes. The corresponding policy for dealing with the `DynamoDB` tables needs to be updated in the `Policies` section. The `CodeUri` section needs to be updated with the S3 URI of the code package.

5. It is to be noted that the meta information should always be included for all SAM, which includes the `AWSTemplateFormatVersion` and `Transform`. This would tell `CloudFormation` that the code you have written is an AWS SAM code and a serverless application. The two lines are as follows:

```
AWSTemplateFormatVersion: '2010-09-09'
Transform: AWS::Serverless-2016-10-31
```

6. If your serverless function needs to access a single table of `DynamoDB`, you can start by creating a `DynamoDB` table via your SAM function itself using the `SimpleTable` attribute. This can be done as follows:

```
AWSTemplateFormatVersion: '2010-09-09'
Transform: AWS::Serverless-2016-10-31
Resources:
    < TableName >:
        Type: AWS::Serverless::SimpleTable
        Properties:
            PrimaryKey:
                Name: id
                Type: String
            ProvisionedThroughput:
                ReadCapacityUnits: 5
                WriteCapacityUnits: 5
```

7. Now, we will learn how to create a Lambda function with a trigger. As we are already using `DynamoDB` for the examples, we will use the same as a trigger in this step. The SAM code for this would look as follows:

```
AWSTemplateFormatVersion: '2010-09-09'
Transform: AWS::Serverless-2016-10-31
Resources:
    < Name of the function >:
        Type: AWS::Serverless::Function
        Properties:
```

```
            Handler: index.handler
            Runtime: < runtime >
            Events:
                Stream:
                    Type: DynamoDB
                    Properties:
                        Stream: !GetAtt DynamoDBTable.StreamArn
                        BatchSize: 100
                        StartingPosition: TRIM_HORIZON
< Name of the table >:
    Type: AWS::DynamoDB::Table
    Properties:
        AttributeDefinitions:
            - AttributeName: id
              AttributeType: S
        KeySchema:
            - AttributeName: id
              KeyType: HASH
        ProvisionedThroughput:
            ReadCapacityUnits: 5
            WriteCapacityUnits: 5
```

CloudFormation for serverless services

In this section, we will learn how CloudFormation can be used to build and deploy Lambda functions. We will do the following:

1. We will write a **CloudFormation** template for a Lambda function that periodically pings a website and gives an error if there is any failure in the process. The **CloudFormation** template for this is as follows:

```
AWSTemplateFormatVersion: '2010-09-09'
Transform: 'AWS::Serverless-2016-10-31'
Description: 'Performs a periodic check of the given site,
erroring out on test failure.'
Resources:
lambdacanary:
    Type: 'AWS::Serverless::Function'
    Properties:
        Handler: lambda_function.lambda_handler
        Runtime: python2.7
        CodeUri: .
        Description: >-
            Performs a periodic check of the given site,
erroring out on test failure.
```

```
MemorySize: 128
Timeout: 10
Events:
    Schedule1:
    Type: Schedule
    Properties:
        Schedule: rate(1 minute)
Environment:
    Variables:
        site: 'https://www.google.com/'
        expected: Search site.
```

2. There is a lot of syntax in this CloudFormation snippet. We will now try to understand it in a bit more detail:
    1. In the first three lines that contain the meta details of the Lambda function, we have the following line—`Transform: 'AWS::Serverless-2016-10-31'`. This line is used to define the resources that a user will be using/accessing, through a **CloudFormation** template. As we are using a Lambda function, we have specified it as `Serverless`.
    2. We have also defined the memory size that our function will be using. It is similar to how we learned to view and change the memory settings in the Lambda's console.
    3. `Timeout` is the amount of time the Lambda function can keep retrying before considering the attempt as a failure.

You can also see that we have added environment variables to our Lambda function that will be stored in the Lambda container and used when needed by the system.

Deploying with SAM

In this section, we will learn how to deploy the SAM applications. We have already learned what SAM applications and code look like, so we will learn how to deploy them via AWS CloudFormation:

1. Firstly, let's set up our local environment for deployment purposes, and then start by installing `awscli` from `pip`:

```
(venv) → Desktop pip install awscli
Collecting awscli
  Downloading awscli-1.14.63-py2.py3-none-any.whl (1.2MB)
    100% |████████████████████████████████| 1.2MB 325kB/s
Collecting botocore==1.9.16 (from awscli)
  Downloading botocore-1.9.16-py2.py3-none-any.whl (4.1MB)
    100% |████████████████████████████████| 4.1MB 183kB/s
Collecting colorama<=0.3.7,>=0.2.5 (from awscli)
  Downloading colorama-0.3.7-py2.py3-none-any.whl
Collecting docutils>=0.10 (from awscli)
  Downloading docutils-0.14-py2-none-any.whl (543kB)
    100% |████████████████████████████████| 552kB 404kB/s
Collecting rsa<=3.5.0,>=3.1.2 (from awscli)
  Downloading rsa-3.4.2-py2.py3-none-any.whl (46kB)
    100% |████████████████████████████████| 51kB 637kB/s
Collecting PyYAML<=3.12,>=3.10 (from awscli)
  Downloading PyYAML-3.12.tar.gz (253kB)
    100% |████████████████████████████████| 256kB 835kB/s
Collecting s3transfer<0.2.0,>=0.1.12 (from awscli)
  Downloading s3transfer-0.1.13-py2.py3-none-any.whl (59kB)
    100% |████████████████████████████████| 61kB 204kB/s
Collecting jmespath<1.0.0,>=0.7.1 (from botocore==1.9.16->awscli)
  Downloading jmespath-0.9.3-py2.py3-none-any.whl
Collecting python-dateutil<2.7.0,>=2.1 (from botocore==1.9.16->awscli)
  Downloading python_dateutil-2.6.1-py2.py3-none-any.whl (194kB)
    100% |████████████████████████████████| 194kB 358kB/s
Collecting pyasn1>=0.1.3 (from rsa<=3.5.0,>=3.1.2->awscli)
  Downloading pyasn1-0.4.2-py2.py3-none-any.whl (71kB)
    100% |████████████████████████████████| 71kB 468kB/s
Collecting futures<4.0.0,>=2.2.0; python_version == "2.6" or python_version == "2.7" (from s3transfer<0.2.0,>=0.1.12->awscli)
  Downloading futures-3.2.0-py2-none-any.whl
Collecting six>=1.5 (from python-dateutil<2.7.0,>=2.1->botocore==1.9.16->awscli)
  Downloading six-1.11.0-py2.py3-none-any.whl
Building wheels for collected packages: PyYAML
  Running setup.py bdist_wheel for PyYAML ... done
  Stored in directory: /Users/Dawny33/Library/Caches/pip/wheels/2c/f7/79/13f3a12cd723892437c0cfbde1230ab4d82947ff7b3839a4fc
Successfully built PyYAML
Installing collected packages: jmespath, six, python-dateutil, docutils, botocore, colorama, pyasn1, rsa, PyYAML, futures, s3transfer, awscli
Successfully installed PyYAML-3.12 awscli-1.14.63 botocore-1.9.16 colorama-0.3.7 docutils-0.14 futures-3.2.0 jmespath-0.9.3 pyasn1-0.4.2 python-dateutil-2.6.1 rsa-3.4.2 s3transfer-0.1.13 six-1.11.0
(venv) → Desktop
```

2. Next, you will need to configure your AWS environment using your credentials:

```
(venv) → Desktop aws configure
AWS Access Key ID [****************OP2Q]:
AWS Secret Access Key [****************+WOV]:
Default region name [None]:
Default output format [None]:
```

3. You will need to enter the following details to make sure your AWS environment is successfully configured:
   - Your AWS Access Key
   - Your AWS Secret Key
   - The default region in which you want to operate
   - The default output format in which you want your data

4. Now, let's try to deploy a simple `Hello World` Lambda application via SAM. We will have two code files for this. One is the Python file and the other is the template `yaml` file.

5. We will use the default `Hello World` example for Python, as we are trying to understand how SAM deployments work instead of stressing too much about the code for now. The Python script will be as follows:

```python
import json
print('Loading function')
def lambda_handler(event, context):
    #print("Received event: " + json.dumps(event, indent=2))
    print("value1 = " + event['key1'])
    print("value2 = " + event['key2'])
    print("value3 = " + event['key3'])
    return event['key1'] # Echo back the first key value
    #raise Exception('Something went wrong')
```

6. We will use a basic template `yaml` file for the SAM function too, whose only job is to define its meta information and to run the Python script that is mentioned previously. The template `yaml` file will look like this:

```yaml
AWSTemplateFormatVersion: '2010-09-09'
Transform: 'AWS::Serverless-2016-10-31'
Description: A starter AWS Lambda function.
Resources:
    helloworldpython3:
        Type: 'AWS::Serverless::Function'
        Properties:
            Handler: lambda_function.lambda_handler
            Runtime: python3.6
            CodeUri: .
            Description: A starter AWS Lambda function.
            MemorySize: 128
            Timeout: 3
```

7. Now, we will package the SAM template we just created, using the command line. The instructions for packaging the code are as follows:

```
aws cloudformation package --template-file template.yaml --output-template-file output.yaml --s3-bucket receiver-bucket
```

You get the following output:

```
(venv) → SAM
(venv) → SAM
(venv) → SAM
(venv) → SAM aws cloudformation package --template-file template.yaml --output-template-file output.yaml --s3-bucket receiver-bucket
Uploading to 22067de83ab3b7a12a153fbd0517d6cf  670 / 670.0  (100.00%)
Successfully packaged artifacts and wrote output template to file output.yaml.
Execute the following command to deploy the packaged template
aws cloudformation deploy --template-file /Users/                           'SAM/output.yaml --stack-name <YOUR STACK NAME>
(venv) → SAM
(venv) → SAM
(venv) → SAM
```

8. This will create an output `yaml` file that needs to be deployed, as mentioned in the preceding trace. The `output.yaml` file looks like this:

```
AWSTemplateFormatVersion: '2010-09-09'
Description: A starter AWS Lambda function.
Resources:
    helloworldpython3:
        Properties:
            CodeUri: s3://receiver-
bucket/22067de83ab3b7a12a153fbd0517d6cf
            Description: A starter AWS Lambda function.
            Handler: lambda_function.lambda_handler
            MemorySize: 128
            Runtime: python3.6
            Timeout: 3
        Type: AWS::Serverless::Function
Transform: AWS::Serverless-2016-10-31
```

9. Now, as we have packaged the SAM template, we will now deploy it. We will use the instructions shown in the trace when we did the packaging for the deployment process. The instructions for deployment are as follows:

```
aws cloudformation deploy --template-file
/Users/<path>/SAM/output.yaml --stack-name 'TestSAM' --
capabilities CAPABILITY_IAM
```

This will give you the following output:

```
(venv) → SAM
(venv) → SAM
(venv) → SAM aws cloudformation deploy --template-file /Users/                    SAM/output.yaml --stack-name 'TestSAM' --capabilities CAPAB
ILITY_IAM
Waiting for changeset to be created..
Waiting for stack create/update to complete
Successfully created/updated stack - TestSAM
(venv) → SAM
```

10. We can head over to the **CloudFormation** console to look at the template we just deployed. The deployed template will look something like this:

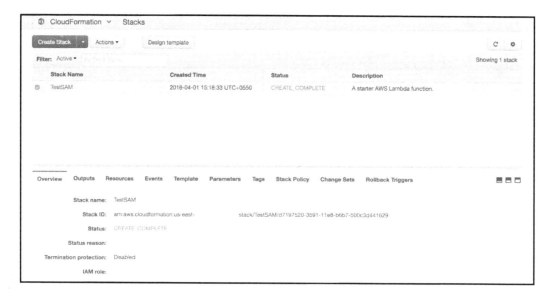

11. In the **Template** tab shown here, we can see both the original template and the processed template. The original template can be seen by selecting the first radio button:

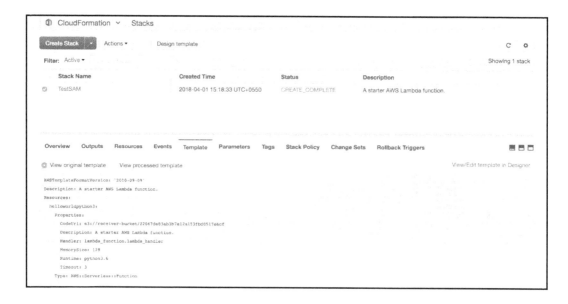

12. The processed template can be seen by selecting the second radio button under the **Template** tab at the bottom:

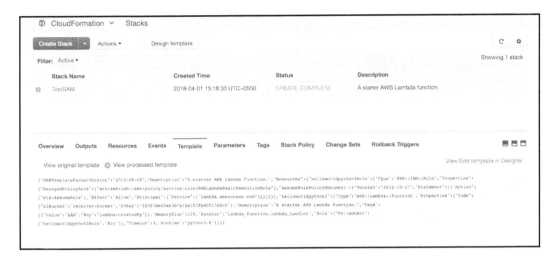

13. If we head over to the **Lambda** console, we will see the newly created Lambda function via SAM with the corresponding name given:

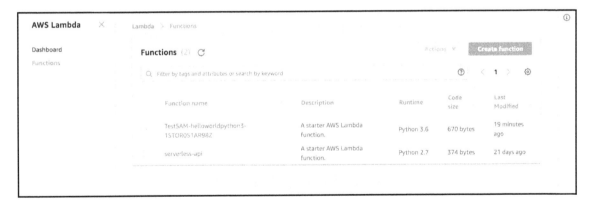

14. Clicking on the **Functions** will give us more information about it. It also mentions the SAM template and the **CloudFormation** template from which it was created:

15. Let's create basic tests for the Lambda function. The test creation console can be opened by clicking on the **Test** button:

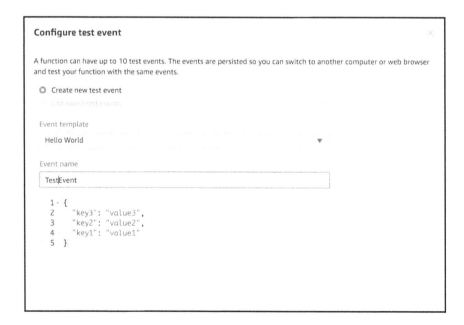

16. Now, once the tests have been created, you can again click on the **Test** button. This will run the testing with the updated test cases. The logs from a successful run will look like this:

17. Now, let's go through each component of the Lambda function properly. The **Configuration** shows the triggers and the logging settings of our Lambda function. We are logging into the CloudWatch service of AWS:

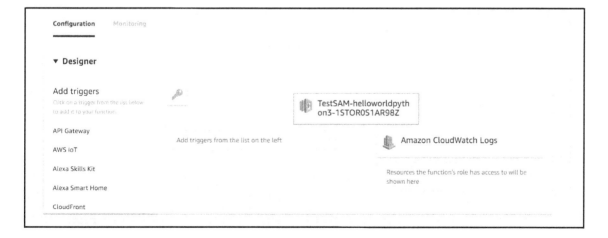

18. We can also see the invocation metrics in the **Monitoring** option in the **Lambda** console. We can see exactly one Lambda invocation:

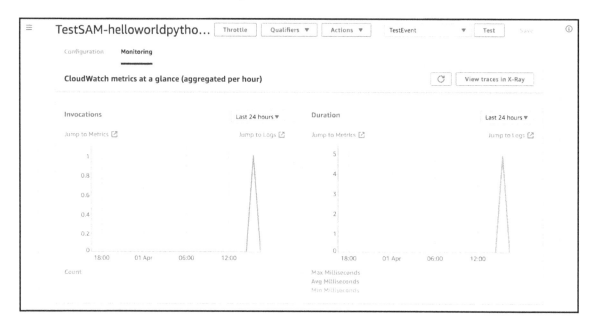

19. You can see the code files in the **Function code** section. You can see the folder structure in the left-hand corner of the interactive code editor that contains both the `template.yaml` file and the function code:

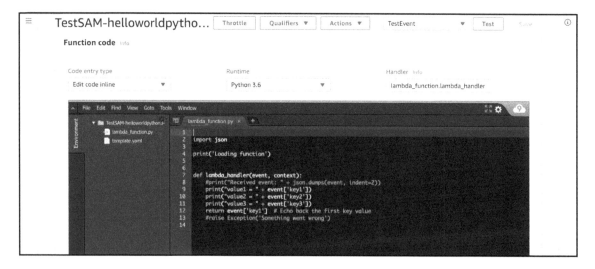

20. And further below, you can see the pre-existing environment variable named `lambda:createdBy`, and also the timeout setting we mentioned in our template.

Understanding security in SAM

So far, we have learned how to write, build, package, and deploy Lambda functions using the SAM. We will now understand how security works inside them:

1. You can scroll to the bottom of the Lambda console to see the network and security settings, where the VPC and the subnet details are mentioned:

2. Now, we will add in the network settings, which include the security groups and the subnet IDs:

```
AWSTemplateFormatVersion: '2010-09-09'
Transform: 'AWS::Serverless-2016-10-31'
Description: A starter AWS Lambda function.
Resources:
    helloworldpython3:
        Type: 'AWS::Serverless::Function'
        Properties:
            Handler: lambda_function.lambda_handler
            Runtime: python3.6
            CodeUri: .
            Description: A starter AWS Lambda function.
            MemorySize: 128
            Timeout: 3
            VpcConfig:
                SecurityGroupIds:
                    - sg-9a19c5ec
                SubnetIds:
                    - subnet-949564de
```

3. Now, package and deploy the newly updated SAM template like we did in the previous section:

```
(venv) → SAM vim template.yaml
(venv) → SAM aws cloudformation package --template-file template.yaml --output-template-file output.yaml --s3-bucket receiver-bucket
Uploading to f94a786f2b5b4a8d25bbf5da5a6c7527  1158 / 1158.0  (100.00%)
Successfully packaged artifacts and wrote output template to file output.yaml.
Execute the following command to deploy the packaged template
aws cloudformation deploy --template-file /Users/Dawny33/Desktop/Work/ServerlessBook/SAM/output.yaml --stack-name <YOUR_STACK_NAME>
(venv) → SAM
(venv) → SAM
(venv) → SAM aws cloudformation deploy --template-file /Users/Dawny33/Desktop/Work/ServerlessBook/SAM/output.yaml --stack-name 'TestSAMSec' --capabilities CA
PABILITY_IAM
Waiting for changeset to be created..
Waiting for stack create/update to complete
Successfully created/updated stack - TestSAMSec
```

4. Now you will see the corresponding network and security settings, once you have packaged and deployed the **CloudFormation** template after the corresponding edits. The **Network** section looks as follows:

5. You can also see the inbound rules of your corresponding security groups that are linked with the VPC in your **Network** settings:

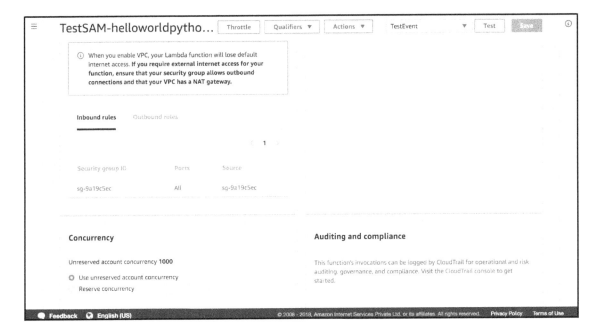

6. You can also see the completed **CloudFormation** template in your console with the updated network and security settings, which means that deployment has been successful:

7. You can also see the original template under the **Templates** option in the bottom corner of the console:

8. The processed template can be found by selecting the **View processed template** option beside the original template option at the bottom of the console:

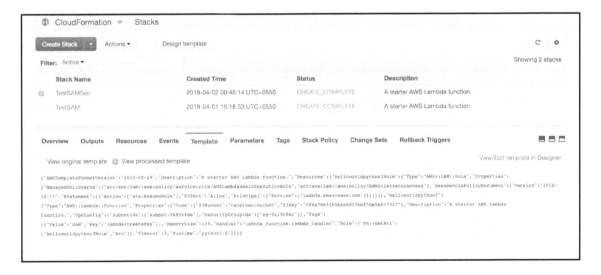

Summary

In this chapter, we learned how to deploy Lambda functions as infrastructure as code via SAM, which is a new way of writing and deploying Lambda functions. This makes it easier to integrate with other IaaS services, such as CloudFormation. We also learned about the AWS CloudFormation service, which is the service that allows and facilitates infrastructure as code. We also learned how security works inside SAM code and how to configure VPC and subnet settings.

In the next chapter, you will be introduced to Microsoft Azure functions, along with configuring and understanding the components of the tool.

Introduction to Microsoft Azure Functions

9

So far, we have learned how to build serverless functions and serverless architectures using Python in the AWS environment. We have also learned about the settings and environment of the AWS Lambda tool in great detail. We shall now learn and explore its counterpart from Microsoft Azure Functions.

In this chapter, you will learn how Microsoft Azure Functions work, what the Microsoft Azure Functions console looks like, and how to go about understanding the settings in the console. This chapter is divided into the following sections:

- Introduction to Microsoft Azure Functions
- Creating your first Azure Function
- Understanding triggers
- Understanding logging and monitoring
- Best practices for writing Microsoft Azure Functions

Introduction to Microsoft Azure Functions

Microsoft Azure Functions is the Azure counterpart of AWS's Lambda service. In this section, we will learn how to locate and navigate the Microsoft Azure Functions console. So, let's start by performing the following steps:

1. You can locate the Azure Functions app by navigating to the **All services** tab on the left menu and typing out the function filter. You will now notice the Microsoft Azure Function's service under the name, **Function Apps**:

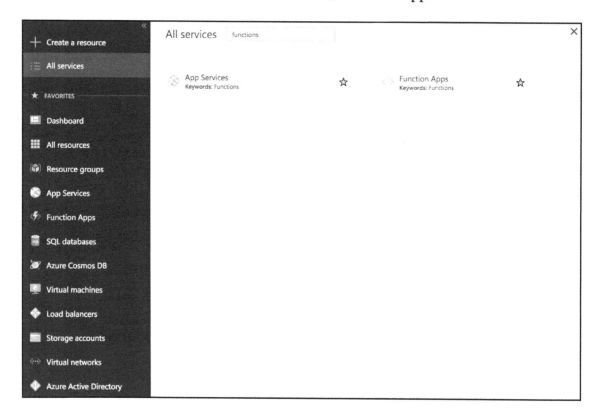

2. Once you click on that, you will be re-directed to the **Function Apps** console. For now, it will be empty if you haven't created any functions. The console will look something like this:

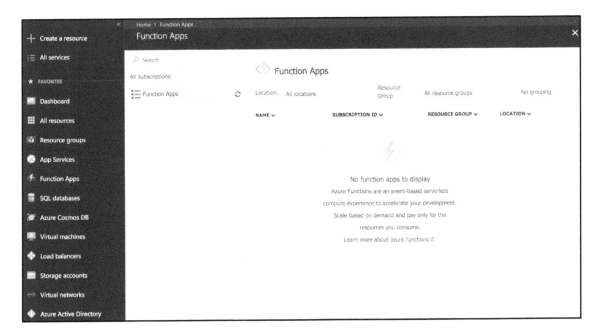

3. Now, let's start with creating an Azure Function. To do so, we need to click on the **Create a resource** option on the left menu, then click on the **Compute** option from that list, and then select the **Function App** option from the subsequent list of options:

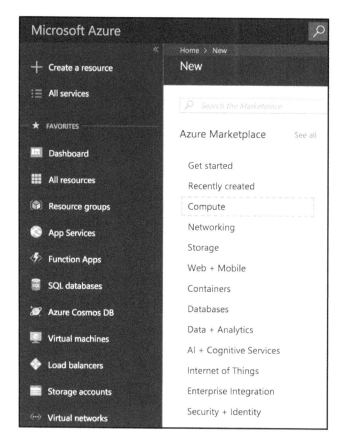

Microsoft Azure Functions come under the list of **Compute** resources on the dashboard. In the following sections, we will learn how to create Microsoft Azure Functions and also understand the different kinds of triggers and how they work.

Creating your first Azure Function

In this section, we will learn how to create and deploy an Azure Function. We will go through the process step by step in order to understand how each section of an Azure function works:

1. When you click on the **Functions App** in the menu, you will be re-directed to the **Function App** creation wizard, as shown in the following screenshot:

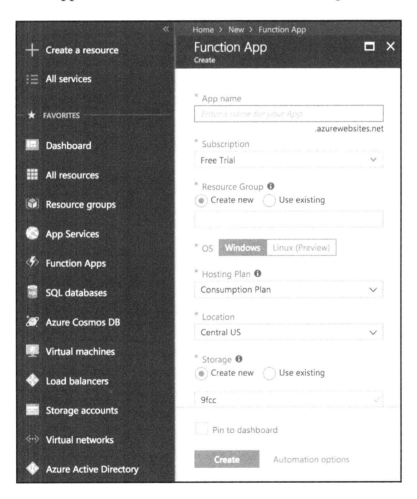

2. Add the required information in the wizard accordingly. Choose **Linux (Preview)** as the OS. Then, click on the blue **Create** button at the bottom of the wizard:

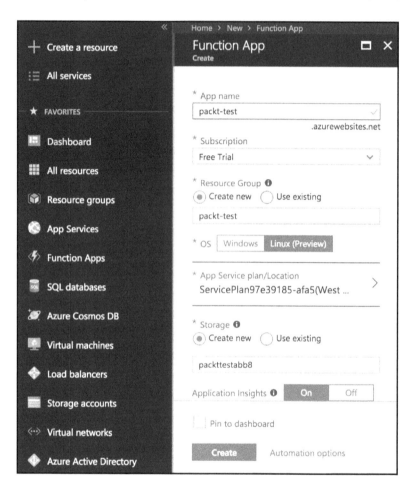

3. Clicking on the **Automation options** at the bottom will open up a validation screen for automating Function deployments. This is not needed for this chapter. This will simply validate your Azure Function:

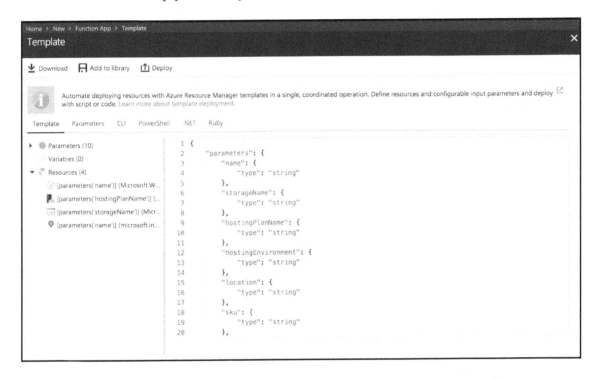

4. Once you click **Create**, you will see the deployment in progress under the **Notifications** menu:

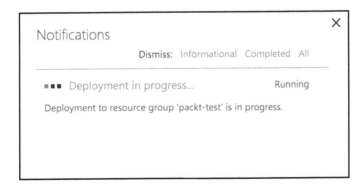

5. Once it has been successfully created, it will be reflected in your notifications list with a green-colored notification:

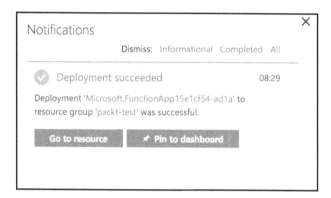

6. Clicking on **Go to resource** will take you to the newly created Azure Function. The function console will look like this:

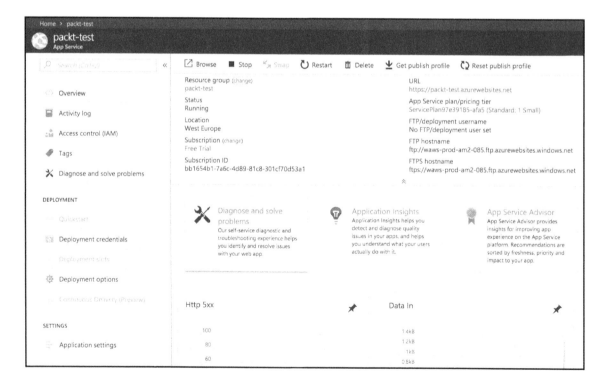

We have successfully created an Azure Function. We will cover in more detail triggers, monitoring, and security in the forthcoming sections of this chapter.

Understanding triggers

In this section, we will look at how triggers work in Azures Function applications. We will also learn about the different types of triggers and their purpose. Perform the following steps:

1. In the left menu, click on the (+) symbol beside the **Functions** option for adding, removing, or editing a trigger:

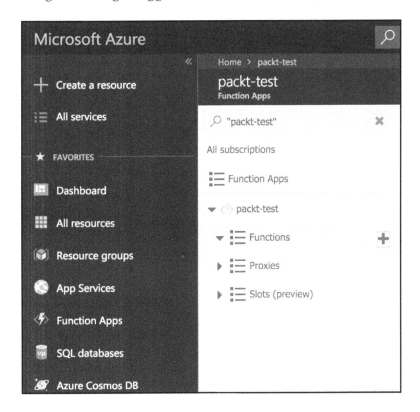

2. You will be taken to the function creation console, which looks like this:

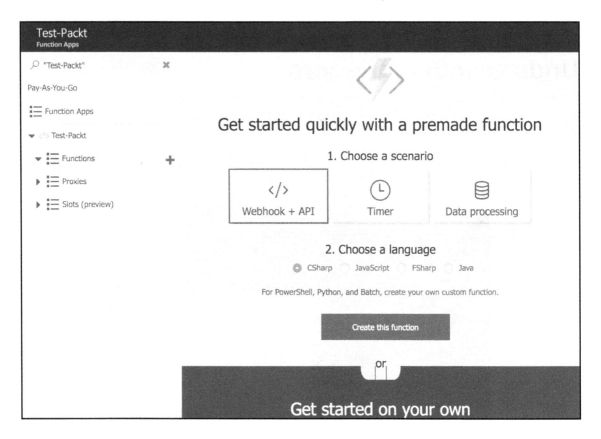

3. Azure does not have a lot of support for Python. So, in this console, let's choose a custom function of our own. Click on **Custom function** under the **Get Started on your own** option at the bottom:

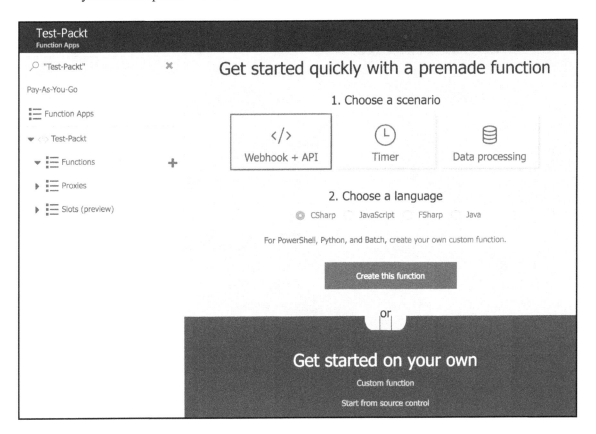

4. In the function creation wizard, enable the **Experimental Language** option in the right menu. Now, you will be able to see the **Python** option in the available languages:

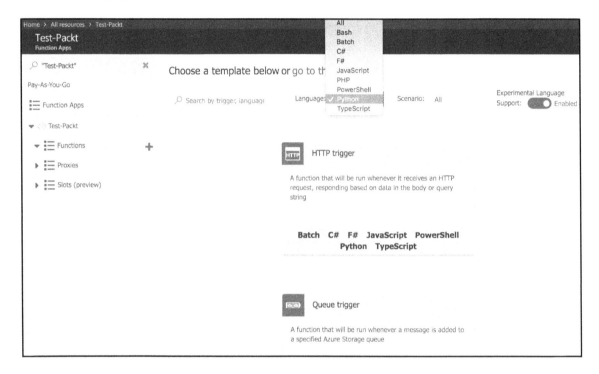

5. There are two triggers that are available for the Python language. One is the **HTTP trigger** and the other is the **Queue trigger**, as seen in the following screenshot:

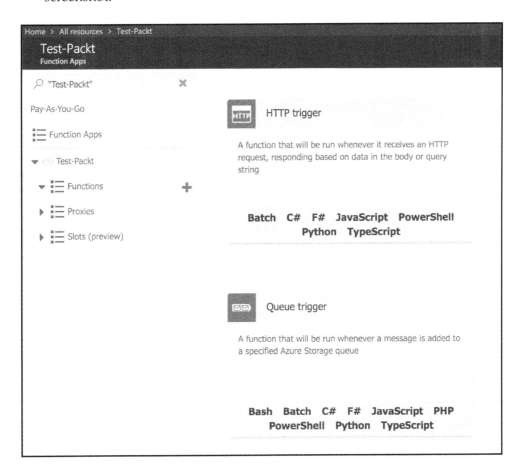

6. The **HTTP trigger** will trigger the function whenever it receives an HTTP request. When you click on it, you will notice options for adding different HTTP-related settings, such as authorization and name:

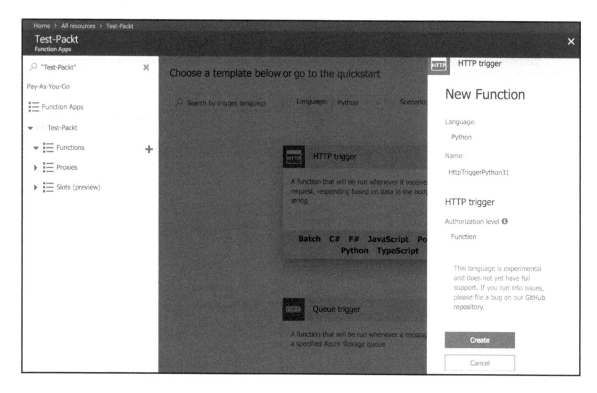

7. The next trigger is the **Queue trigger**. This will trigger the function whenever a message is added to the queue. We have done the same in AWS Lambda in one of our previous chapters too:

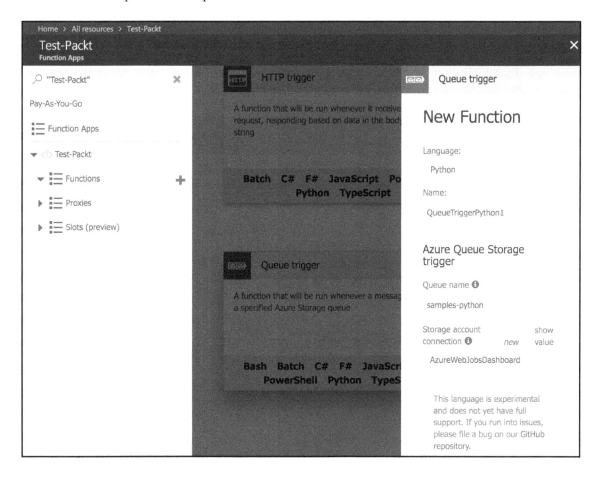

Understanding logging and monitoring in Azures Functions

In this section, we will learn and understand the monitoring and logging mechanisms available to the user in Microsoft Azure Functions. Perform the following steps:

1. By clicking on the **Monitor** option under the function, we can access the monitoring suite of that particular Azure Function:

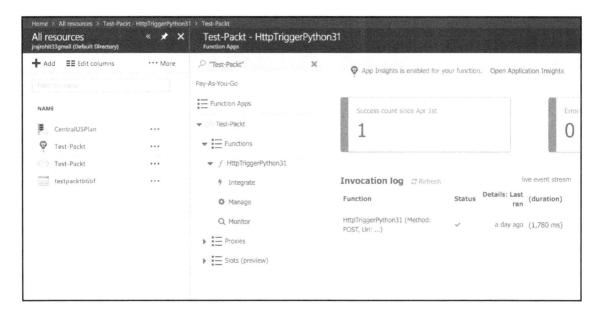

2. The monitoring suite for the function that we created looks like this:

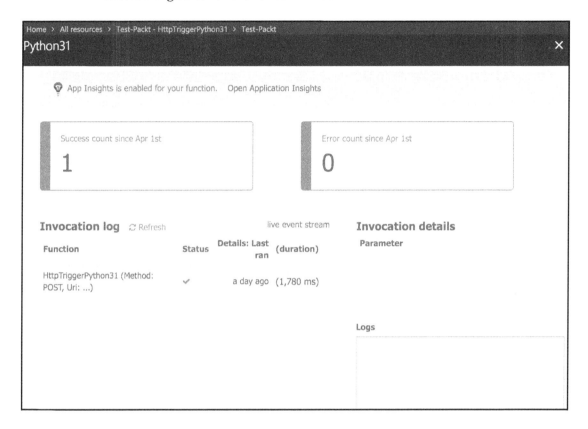

3. Now, click on the **Open Application Insights** option at the top of the menu. This will take you to the detailed monitoring page:

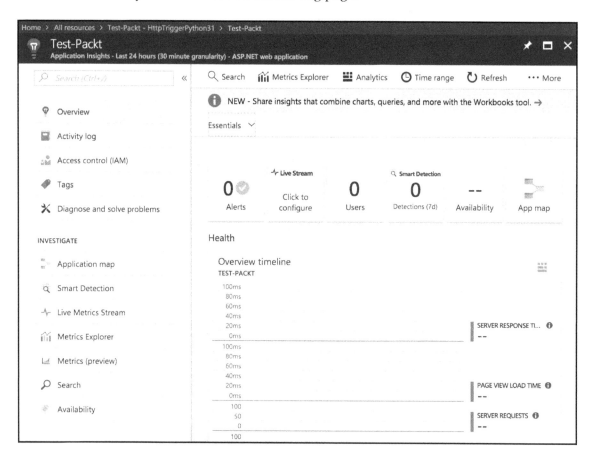

4. If you scroll down, you will see the function-specific metrics, such as the server response times and request performance. This is very useful as it means we don't need separate dashboards for monitoring all these statistics:

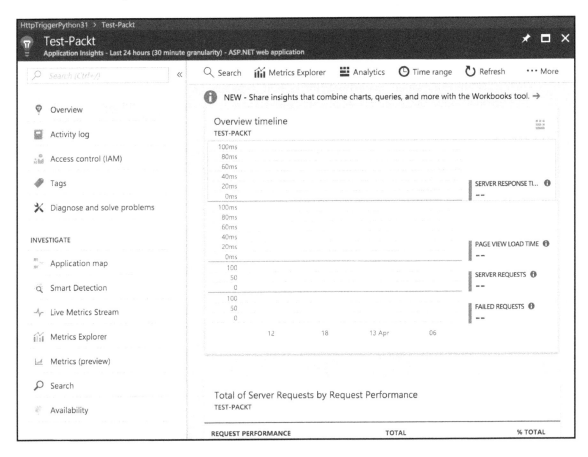

Now that we have learned about Microsoft Azure Functions logging and monitoring, let's go through some best practices.

Best practices for writing Azure Functions

We have learned how to create, configure, and deploy Microsoft Azure Functions. We will now learn about the best practices for using them:

- Microsoft Azure Functions don't have a huge support for Python like AWS Lambda. They have a very limited set of Python-based triggers. So, you need to write custom functions for most of them. Developers need to keep that in mind before taking a decision on using Microsoft Azure Functions. The languages supported by Microsoft Azure Functions are **C#**, **F#**, and **JavaScript**:

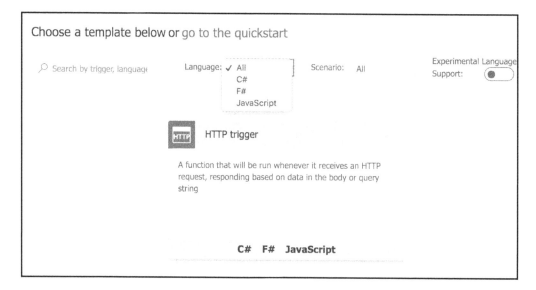

- The experimental languages that are supported by Microsoft Azure Functions are **Bash**, **Batch**, **PHP**, **TypeScript**, **Python**, and **PowerShell**:

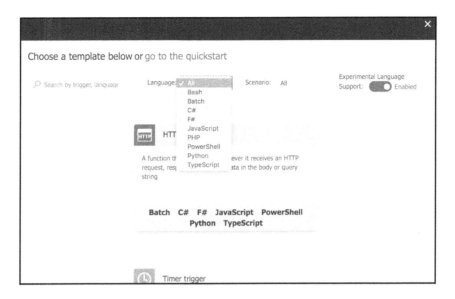

- Make sure you use the security settings properly to secure your functions. You can find all the settings you need in the **Platform features** options:

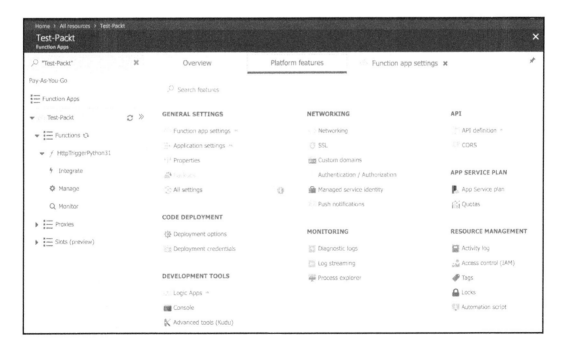

- Finally, use monitoring as much as possible, as it is crucial to log and monitor serverless functions. We have already gone through the monitoring details and the corresponding settings.

Summary

In this chapter, we learned about Microsoft Azure Functions and how to build them. We learned about the various functionalities available, along with the available triggers for the Python runtime. We also learned and experimented with the logging and monitoring capabilities of Microsoft Azure Functions along with understanding and experimenting with the experimental features of Azure such as the additional runtimes apart from the standard set of languages it offers out of the box.

Other Books You May Enjoy

If you enjoyed this book, you may be interested in these other books by Packt:

Serverless computing in Azure with .NET
Sasha Rosenbaum

ISBN: 978-1-78728-839-3

- Understand the best practices of Serverless architecture
- Learn how how to deploy a Text Sentiment Evaluation application in an Azure Serverless environment
- Implement security, identity, and access control
- Take advantage of the speed of deployment in the cloud
- Configure application health monitoring, logging, and alerts
- Design your application to ensure cost effectiveness, high availability, and scale

Building Serverless Architectures
Cagatay Gurturk

ISBN: 978-1-78712-919-1

- Learn to form microservices from bigger Softwares
- Orchestrate and scale microservices
- Design and set up the data flow between cloud services and custom business logic
- Get to grips with cloud provider's APIs, limitations, and known issues
- Migrate existing Java applications to a serverless architecture
- Acquire deployment strategies
- Build a highly available and scalable data persistence layer
- Unravel cost optimization techniques

Leave a review - let other readers know what you think

Please share your thoughts on this book with others by leaving a review on the site that you bought it from. If you purchased the book from Amazon, please leave us an honest review on this book's Amazon page. This is vital so that other potential readers can see and use your unbiased opinion to make purchasing decisions, we can understand what our customers think about our products, and our authors can see your feedback on the title that they have worked with Packt to create. It will only take a few minutes of your time, but is valuable to other potential customers, our authors, and Packt. Thank you!

Index

working 62, 63, 64, 66, 67, 68, 69, 70, 72, 73, 74
SQS trigger
  about 75
  working 76, 78, 80, 82, 83, 84, 85
STS
  using, inside Lambda for secure session-based execution 213

T

third-party orchestration tools
  Ansible 174, 176, 177
  Chef 170, 172

triggers
  working 243, 245, 246, 247, 248, 249

U

user controls
  handling 120, 121, 122, 123, 124, 125, 126, 127

V

Version Control System (VCS) 39
Virtual Private Cloud (VPCs)
  about 176, 196, 198, 199, 200, 201, 202
  subnets 203, 204, 206, 207

www.ingramcontent.com/pod-product-compliance
Lightning Source LLC
Chambersburg PA
CBHW080633060326
40690CB00021B/4913